Influencing Your World FOR Christ

Influencing Your World for Christ:

Practical

Everyday

Evangelism

Matthew Robert Payne

This book is copyrighted by Matthew Robert Payne. Copyright © 2016. All rights reserved.

No part of this publication may be reproduced, stored in a retrieval system or transmitted in any way by any means, electronic, mechanical, photocopy, recording or otherwise, without the prior permission of the author except as provided by USA copyright law.

To sow into Matthew's writing ministry, to request a personal prophecy or life coaching or to contact him, please visit http://personal-prophecy-today.com.

This book was edited by Lisa Thompson. You can email her at writebylisa@gmail.com or visit her website at www.writebylisa.com.

Cover designed by akira007 at fiverr.com.

Unless otherwise indicated, all Scripture taken from the New King James Version. Copyright © 1982 by Thomas Nelson, Inc. Used by permission. All rights reserved.

Scripture quotations are taken from the Holy Bible, New Living Translation, copyright ©1996, 2004, 2007, 2013, 2015 by Tyndale House Foundation. Used by permission of Tyndale House Publishers, Inc., Carol Stream, Illinois 60188. All rights reserved.

The opinions expressed by the author are not necessarily those of Revival Waves of Glory Books & Publishing.

Published by Revival Waves of Glory Books & Publishing PO Box 596| Litchfield, Illinois 62056 USA www.revivalwavesofgloryministries.com.

Revival Waves of Glory Books & Publishing is committed to excellence in the publishing industry. Book design Copyright © 2016 by Revival Waves of Glory Books & Publishing. All rights reserved.

Paperback: 978-1-68411-186-2

Hardcover: 978-1-68411-187-9

Table of Contents

Dedication viii

Acknowledgments ix

A Word from My Editor xi

Introduction xiii

The Church Should Go to the People 1

Become Salt and Light! 5

What Does Light Do? 11

How to Become Salt in Your Community 14

Encouraging Others 21

Building Up People 25

Being a Positive Voice 28

Bringing Joy to Others 32

Not Speaking Ill of People 36

Sharing Your Struggles with People 39

Being Transparent 43

Sharing Your Faith in Normal Conversations 49

Actively Listening to People 54

Remember to Follow Up 57

Taking an Interest in Their Interests 61

Be a Friend without Expecting Anything in Return 65

Give Them Time 70

Friendship with no Agenda but to Be Jesus to Them 72

Support During Times of Trouble 76

Actively Help when Difficulties Come 79

Learn how to Lead a Person to Christ 81

Daily Prayers for People God Brings Across Your Path 85

Learn to Prophesy or Heal 87

Invite Your Friends to Evangelistic Outreaches 92

Give Powerful Books to Your Friends 94

Simply Share the Gospel 98

Read Resources on how to Share the Gospel 101

Pray from Your Friend's Perspective 102

Introduce your Friends to Other Christians 104

Include Them in Your Christian Groups 106

Ask God to Open Your Friend's Heart to Your Faith 109

When They Make a Decision for Jesus, Disciple Them 110

Closing Thoughts 115

I'd love to hear from you 118

About the Author 122

Dedication

I dedicate this book to my sister, Carmen, who has modeled being the light and salt in people's lives. She has a wonderful heart and is longsuffering when it comes to her friends. Everyone needs a friend like my sister.

Acknowledgments

Father God

I want to thank you for loving me, for leading me and for making me into the person that I am today.

Jesus Christ

Thank you for being my Friend for all of my life. You have led me and trained me, and you have allowed me to write some encouraging books. You are a joy to me. You introduced me to your Father, and now, I am getting to know him better through the years.

Lisa Thompson

I want to thank you for polishing my words and making this book a better book. You take my simple language and make it more readable and understandable. I want to thank you for working on so many books with me.

If you need editing services, you can contact Lisa at her website at www.writebylisa.com or directly via email at writebylisa@gmail.com.

Bill Vincent

I want to thank Bill Vincent, who produces my paperback books, my e-books and my audio books. His company, Revival Waves of Glory Books & Publishing, has shown me great favor, and without you, I would be spending a lot more money to produce books. I give you my heartfelt thanks.

The readers

I want to thank my readers. You have motivated me to write this. I hope that you really enjoy it and that many of you put what I have said into practice. I am no expert at this, but I am the very best that I can be.

June Payne

I want to thank my mother for being love to me and an example of patience and understanding.

A Word from My Editor

I had the pleasure of editing this book for Matthew. This is the eighth book that we have worked on together, which has given me a unique insight into his life. Although he shares similar stories in each of his books, this one outlines his lifestyle of evangelism the most clearly. Actually, the title sums it up beautifully — he has moved beyond just evangelism as an activity to now "influencing his world for Christ."

In his simple yet practical way, Matthew shares exactly how he has been able to impact thousands of people for Christ through the years. He invites the reader to take a peek into his life and shares ways that they, too, can connect with those around them — in the workplace, their neighbors, roommates, friends and many, many more.

As you open the pages of this book, prepare to be changed! You will be surprised at just how easily you can connect with people on a day-to-day basis and win others to

Christ. I believe that the fruit from this book will be immense as you, dear reader, take these ideas and apply them to your own life, seeing many salvations as a result.

Enjoy your new adventure with God, and happy reading!

Lisa

If you are looking for an editor, I would love to connect with you. You can visit my website at www.writebylisa.com or email me directly at writebylisa@gmail.com.

Introduction

1 Corinthians 3:7-9 New Living Translation

"It's not important who does the planting, or who does the watering. What's important is that God makes the seed grow. The one who plants and the one who waters work together with the same purpose. And both will be rewarded for their own hard work. For we are both God's workers. And you are God's field. You are God's building."

As Christians, one of the most alarming things that can happen to us is to see a friend or relative of ours die without giving their life to Jesus. It is heartbreaking, and if that has ever happened to you, the mere mention of it here will cause you anguish.

I know that all of us would love to know how to evangelize our friends and family, yet so few of us feel qualified to do so. Many of us pray earnestly for the people we love but feel powerless to share the Gospel with them.

According to a study by Lifeway Research, about half of all Christians in the USA have never brought an unsaved person to church.[1] As the author of 20 books to my credit, I wanted to add a simple book to my catalogue for any of you that want to learn how I do life with people.

To me, sharing my faith is easy, but you might struggle with talking about Jesus to others. The life that I live in Christ, along with the related skills, has been hard fought and won over many years. To me, what I have written is pretty simple, but as easy as it sounds, you will need to apply these truths for them to be effective.

I encourage you all to read, study and put some of these truths that I have shared into practice in your life. It might be that you are doing many of these things already. If that is so, I hope that you will feel very encouraged and edified by this book.

Please rest assured that if you only plant seeds with your life and relationships, and if you only water those seeds, that God, in his mercy, will raise up someone to bring in the harvest for you when the time is right. I wish that I was in your city so that you could invite me to come and have dinner with your non-Christian friend.

I took a week to record the five videos that this book is taken from, yet it took me 40 years to become the person that

---

[1] http://www.lifeway.com/Article/research-survey-sharing-christ-2012. Accessed Nov. 7, 2016.

could sit down and record them. I don't quote many Bible verses in this book, but I do mention a few resources that I encourage you to obtain.

I pray that you will enjoy what I have to say and recommend of this book to your friends in person, on Facebook and on other social media channels.

May God bless you.

Matthew Robert Payne

November 2016

The Church Should Go to the People Instead of Expecting the People to Go to the Church

When Jesus said "Go into all the world" in the Great Commission, he didn't mean for you to go to church, stay there and expect other people to be automatically attracted to your church and come there to be saved. Jesus didn't teach this model. When he trained his disciples, he sent them into each town to heal the sick and cast out demons and preach the Kingdom. He told them to find a noble person, a person of repute in that town, and to stay at that person's house; then, he said to lay hands on the sick and cast out demons and preach the Gospel and tell them that the Kingdom had come near. So what were they doing? They were casting out demons from people, and they were healing the sick. When people were amazed at what they were doing, then they were sharing, "This is the Kingdom of Jesus! This is how Jesus operates!"

Wouldn't the world be amazing if we had more people with the ability to heal? I have a good friend on Facebook. I know him from his website, from his podcasts, his blog and from his books. His pen name is Praying Medic. He has written a book called, "Divine Healing made Simple," which teaches people how to develop the gift of healing. Healing is something that has a shock and awe factor to it. If someone's limping along with a sore leg because of damage in their knee, and if you come alongside them and ask if you can pray for them, you will shock them. If you lay hands on them and that damage in the leg gets healed so that they no longer suffer with pain, this really has a drastic effect on people. That really demonstrates Christ within you.

Many people are learning how to heal today. I am still in process. I'm gifted in the prophetic. I can reach out to people by sharing prophecies with them. The Great Commission doesn't tell us to go to church each Sunday and worship at church and expect other people to come to church. We are first encouraged to go out into the whole world and share the Gospel, the good news of Jesus Christ, with the people of the world.

Now, the good news of Jesus Christ isn't really about giving your life to Jesus so that you won't go to hell. It's a more complete message than that, which says that we should become everything that we're meant to be through getting to know the Creator of the universe and getting to know what we're created to do. That's a more holistic example of what

Jesus can do. Of course, for you to be able to demonstrate that Gospel, you need to do what you're created to do. You need to be actively pursuing what you are born to do.

People in this world are looking for a purpose and reason to live. So much of the purpose of living is found in Christ and so much of what we are born to do can be found in a relationship with him. God doesn't want you to stay in church. Some people who want to be in full-time Christian ministry are essentially saying that they want to only be around Christians.

God has arranged it so that people have jobs in secular society among non-Christians because he wants you to share the flavor and aroma of Christ among people who don't smell that aroma. He wants you to share his love, his joy, his peace, his comfort and his understanding with people who are devoid of that. The Great Commission is a calling for us to go out and mix with the people of the world and demonstrate Jesus and his love and compassion to people in the world. It doesn't mean just going to church each Sunday. Church attendance each Sunday and going to Bible study once a week isn't fulfilling the Great Commission.

This book isn't intended to be a guilt trip or to condemn you for not reaching out. Instead, it's a book that I hope will demonstrate "how to be Christ in your community." It's how to be salt and light. It will show you how to reflect Jesus and how to live a life so that people you know will have a chance to understand the Gospel and to meet Jesus.

෴✦ෆ

Become Salt and Light!

We'll go to a Scripture that talks about that in Mathew 5:13-16.

"You are the salt of the earth; but if the salt loses its flavor, how shall it be seasoned? It is then good for nothing but to be thrown out and trampled underfoot by men. You are the light of the world. A city that is set on a hill cannot be hidden. Nor do they light a lamp and put it under a basket, but on a lamp stand, and it gives light to all who are in the house. Let your light so shine before men, that they may see your good works and glorify your Father in heaven."

What does salt look like? Salt has two commonly understood properties. In days gone by, before refrigerators, they used to pat down meat with salt as a way of preserving the meat and stopping it from spoiling. Salt also provides flavor. Salt actually doesn't just add flavoring but accentuates the existing flavor in food.

What does light do? In society, the world that we live in is fast losing its morals; it's fast declining and becoming more and more wretched. At the moment, it's considered a sin and unhealthy for a pedophile to have sex with a child. However, a time might be coming in the federal courts in America where this will be looked at and accepted as a natural inclination of a man.

Gay and lesbian couples can now legally marry, according to the 2015 Supreme Court decision. For 2000 years since Christ, marriage was accepted as a practice between a male and a female. However, now, homosexual marriage is accepted as the norm and approved by the Supreme Court in the U.S. Talk is rumbling of legalizing marriage between people in a threesome relationship of mixed genders.

The perversions of society are growing steadily and steadily worse. As Christians, our job is to be the preserver of society. When people are discussing subjects and asking our opinions, we can respond with kindness and understanding. We can tell them that we believe that marriage is between a male and a female and that we love and have compassion for people who are gay. They should have some other label instead of calling the relationship marriage because marriage is between a man and a woman. You have to understand and know about these issues and be prepared to lovingly share in the times that we live in.

People want to know if it's okay to spend 30 minutes on Facebook while they are at work and on company time. Your coworkers need to see that you don't do that; they need to see that you are working when you're on company time. Let them see that the only time you check your Facebook and interact with others is on your break.

However, someone who is salt wouldn't spend a lot of time on Facebook during their break. They would instead talk to other staff and interact with them, engaging them in friendly conversation. People are looking to us for a standard. They are not looking to us to be judged; they are not coming to us to hear our decision or our critiques on certain topics. They are looking to us to set a standard just like a child knows what limits and lines to cross with their parents.

When parents set clear boundaries, the child feels comfortable and at ease and knows not to cross those boundaries. The same is true with society. Our society needs standards, and when these standards are taken away, people are unhappy. People assume that a life of debauchery and a life of sin is more enjoyable, but they don't realize that the laws and standards that society has keep the peace, joy and order reigning.

People need to know that we need standards, and we need to stick to our word. That doesn't mean that we have to be completely intolerant and judgmental. For instance, I have three gay friends and four lesbian friends at the moment. They all know they are loved by me, and each of them has a Christian faith. A couple of them live together and plan to marry. How do I communicate to them as the "salt" in society?

They understand that I love them, but they understand that I don't believe their lifestyle is okay. Even so, they know I love and accept them. They see my compassion and love every time we meet. In fact, some of them say that I'm one of their favorite people. I think that Jesus demonstrated that he was the friend of sinners, so he was in trouble with the Pharisees for hanging out with sinners — tax-collectors or the equivalent of today's pedophiles.

Publicans, people running bars, prostitutes and sinners of all sorts congregated around Jesus. Jesus loved them and showed them love. That's one aspect of salt as a preserver.

The other aspect of salt is to give something flavor, to make it taste just right. To many people of the world, Christians seem rigid, full of rules, boring, religious and hard to get along with.

Instead, these are ways to describe something that's full of flavor. We should be known for love, joy, peace, kindness, goodness, self-control and compassion. That's the flavor — that's what we need to demonstrate and not just talk about. When people are in a stressful situation, we need to bring peace to that situation. When people are upset, we need to bring joy; when people are out of control, we need to bring order; when people don't have their needs met, we need to bring goodness and kindness and compassion.

We need to be the "glue" that holds society together. Many hospitals, programs for orphans, community outreaches, missionary endeavors and more are done by Christian people. This is an example of the flavor, the way the Christian church in the West can flavor the East. In the impoverished nations, they can come and fulfill the needs of their community through love and care.

We need to be like a pleasant aroma. When a woman wearing a nice perfume walks past a man, he is attracted to her because of the perfume. Women also appreciate a nice cologne on a man. When a woman walks past with a nice perfume on, other women recognize it and wonder what it is, wishing that they had some for themselves. We need to be like that perfume. We need to be something that the world is jealous of and that attracts them to us.

As I began this book, we just endured the terrorist attack in Paris in November 2015. We need to be the voice of reason and of peace; we need to bring comfort; we don't need to be stressed or worried. Instead, we need to be people that are self-assured and that bring reason and strength and support to challenging situations.

We need to demonstrate Jesus Christ. Many people can't reflect him because they don't know who he is. They don't understand who Jesus was. They don't understand or know Jesus. In order to be successful at being a flavor, in order to bring flavor and saltiness to the world, we need to understand who Jesus was. We need to understand that he was someone remarkably different from what people believe. I have a book called "Finding Intimacy with Jesus Made Simple" that addresses the life of Jesus and what sort of person he is. I've got another book called "Jesus Speaking Today" that further goes into the life of Jesus. It would help you to buy those books so that you could have a clear understanding of who Jesus is!

You need to understand what being salt is and who Jesus really was — how he reacted and how he positioned himself and demonstrated 'the love of the Father' to the people on the earth. He didn't just die on the cross, but he laid down his life every day and gave of himself. He went out of his way every day to fulfill the needs of the people that came to him. He was able to meet the financial needs of people who came to him for money. He had rich people giving him money all the time and was always giving away money. Judas was in charge of the money because someone had to be treasurer and look after the funds that came in. As fast as it came in, it flowed out again. I'll leave you to read these other two books of mine so that you can understand who Jesus was. In that way, you can better demonstrate him

What Does Light Do?

When you're lost, light shines and brightens up the way to lead you into safety. Again, to repeat what Scripture says in Matthew 5:14-16: "You are the light of the world. A city that is set on a hill cannot be hidden. Nor do they light a lamp and put it under a basket, but on a lamp stand, and it gives light to all who are in the house. Let your light so shine before men, that they may see your good works and glorify your Father in heaven."

Do people light a lamp and put it under a basket? Many Christians do this. They don't shine their light. However, you are meant to put it on a lamp stand so that it gives light to all that are in the house. Let me illustrate. If you work as a supervisor of people taking calls at a telephone call center, you probably came up through the ranks, handling the calls at some point in time. As a supervisor, you deal with problem calls, solving the matter for the person on the other end of the line with your knowledge, wisdom and authority in that position. Being the light in that situation means being grace, understanding, kindness, goodness, joy, peace, love and compassion to everyone in the building. It means that you are to be the best encourager, the person who listens to and builds up people, the person that goes beyond the call of duty and really demonstrates understanding, compassion and love to the workers that they need from their supervisor.

Of course, the business has rules and regulations, and if people consistently came in late, you would have to speak to them and discipline them and set the necessary boundaries for the workplace. You would have to make sure that people are not crossing the boundaries, but you could have a measure of mercy. For example, you might have an employee who's a single woman with children, and if they get sick so that she needs to stay home with them, you could show her understanding and leniency. To be light is something that's attractive because the light shows you the answer when you're in darkness. As the supervisor, you want happy employees who work to reach the targets and goals that you set. Your kindness motivates them, and they hope that you get your bonus for the month because you are such a beautiful person.

Putting your light on a lampstand to light the whole house doesn't necessarily refer to a house but can refer to your workplace or wherever God puts you in the community. You can be that person in the workplace that listens, cares, doesn't gossip, that finds solutions, that has compassion on people, that's full of mercy with others and who actively tries to help people in their struggles. I'm going to go into more detail as we progress, but being a light is amazing and powerful. We all know that Jesus is the light of this world, but he told us that we're the light of the world also.

He says, in verse 14, you are the light of the world. A city set on a hill cannot be hidden.

Because the Holy Spirit and Christ live in us, we've become the light of the world. We're the ones who should show others the pathway to truth. We're the ones that are meant to have the answers for people. We're the ones that should communicate with God and have the answers that people are seeking. We should be a conduit to God for people.

I'll speak about having a prophetic gift later on and how you can influence the people through the prophetic as a conduit for God.

How to Become Salt in Your Community

What are some ways you can influence your community as salt to others?

One way to do so is to be salt in your workplace. Now, I'm sure that the majority of people who read this book or watch this video are not working in a Christian ministry, a church or a mission organization. Instead, most of you are probably working at a secular company around non-Christians. So how can you be salt in your community?

First of all, be salt, be the flavor, be the preserver in the way you live out your life. Some people complain that they wish they were in a workplace with more Christians because they feel assaulted at work, and people treat them as the enemy. Can I share something with you? I've never seemed to have a problem with the non-Christians — they always seem to love me. That's what's different about me! One of the main reasons that I'm writing this book is because I want to demonstrate how to accomplish that to you. I want to share with you some keys and some concepts about how to be salt in your community.

I'm well known at the local restaurants that I frequent as well as at my local shop and my gas station, both of which are very close to my place. All the workers there know me and love me. They love seeing me and greet me when I come into the store. They don't greet everyone who comes there, but they greet me and say hello.

I take an interest in the workers, asking lots of questions about their day, their work shift, their family and school. My interest shows that I care about them. You can be salt in your community by demonstrating this type of a good flavor, by being Christ at home, to your community and wherever you're planted.

Although everyone doesn't have a full-time job, many people work 8 hours a day, 40 hours a week. You might even spend more time at your job than you spend at home. This is the place where you should have the greatest impact. Of course, you need to be a great influence in your own home, but God wants you to be salt where you're spending 8 hours a day. He wants you to be that flavor and bring Christ's compassion, love, joy, peace, self-control, kindness, goodness and understanding to your job. He wants you to be a friend to the person who feels left out. He wants you to speak up in defense of the person who is maligned because they are Hindu or because they wear a turban or if they are being picked on. He wants you to come alongside them.

Many people think that the Gospel means that you tell everybody that they are sinners and that they are going to burn in hell if they don't do things God's way. Some people are very passionate about the Kingdom and about saving people, but they seem to turn off nearly everybody that they mix with. They are so rigid and so full of religion that everyone seems to hate them. This is not being salt in your community. Of course, if a gay man asks you whether you believe in a gay relationship or in gay marriage and "marriage equality," you should have an answer for him. You can state very plainly that God created Eve for Adam and not another Adam for Adam. You can say that you understand marriage to be between a man and a woman.

You can say that you understand his sexual orientation and his attraction to a male. But you don't have to be rude about it. You can say politely that you don't agree with gay marriage. You can say that you understand the sense of commitment to their love relationship, but you can make your feelings clear. Then, just be loving to that person in their sin. People need to know that you love them, accept them and understand them. Before they are willing to listen to your side or willing to come over to the way you think, people need to know that you accept them. They need to know you love them and understand them before they're willing to hear any different ideas from you. Being salt doesn't mean that you can't express your beliefs or back down on your views about what the Bible says. But being salt is showing compassion, love, kindness, goodness, peace, love, joy and understanding to people.

Jesus loves me despite my sin. He loves me in the midst of my sin. God demonstrated his love for us that while we were still sinners, Christ died for us (Romans 5:8). We need to demonstrate that same understanding, acceptance and love to people who are living in a life of sin. We need to take some time to understand people.

If a lot of Jews are in your workplace, you might take the time to learn how a Jewish person thinks. You can read Jewish literature and get to know their background and beliefs. They serve a holy God who is one and have a different perspective and understanding of God than Christians do. By understanding them, you can now level the playing field. You have a way to reach and impact others. If you are being salt, they are going to know you're a Christian soon enough. Many times, they're going to expect you, as a Christian, to judge them, and when you're not judging them, when they find out that you know a lot about their faith, they're going to be willing to open up to you.

Here's an example. One day, I was walking down the street, and I saw a young girl with a witchcraft pentagram hanging around the neck. I asked her, "Are you a witch?"

She replied, "Yes."

I put my arm around her and said, "I am a Christian, and I love witches!"

That really shocked her. I asked, "Hey, tell me, do you know how to prophesy? Can you tell things about a person, and can you tell them about their future?"

She answered me, "Yeah."

I suggested, "How about if I give you a prophecy, and then, you give me a prophecy?"

She replied, "That sounds great!"

I took my arm from around her shoulders. I said, "This is what you're all about." I went on to tell her about herself, her life, what she likes, what sort of person she is and her future.

When I finished, she was undone with shock. Then, she prophesied over me according to her gift.

When she finished, I thanked her. She reckoned, "I was the coolest Christian she'd ever met." That was the demonstration to her of my salt; that was a demonstration to her of my life.

You are planted in your job, and you're going to be there for a long time. It's time to demonstrate Christ to the people that you're doing life with. Further on, I'll go into details about how you can do that. I'll explain ways that I do it so that you gain some understanding about how to be salt and how to be light.

I know time will pass, and it might be years later, but the Paris attacks seemed to really scare people. The terrorists were let in as refugees, and some of them created active terror in the new country. People are really concerned that if we let refugees into a country, it will be a breeding ground for terrorists and ISIS, and they will attack us and do great damage. People are really afraid. Being light brings the voice of reason and understanding as others search for answers. Not every answer has to be clear cut. Even the leader of an organization or a church might not have all the answers. You just need to be comfortable speaking with others and be a voice of reason. You should have a solid relationship with God and be open to him so that you can receive instruction and direction from him.

People are looking for direction, stability and answers. As I said, you don't have to supply the answer right away but just be the voice of reason. One interesting thing about the world is that people really value their lives, and they are not really sure where they're going to go when they die. What I sense at the moment is this tremendous opportunity for Christians to speak about their assurance of where they will go when they die. Christians have an amazing opportunity to share that they're at peace even if they died in a terrorist attack. They know where they are going, and they are happy to go there.

But people don't share that on Facebook. During the shooting at Columbine High School, one of the shooters asked people if they were Christians. If they said they were, he shot them. The media didn't make much of the courage of those people who confessed that they were Christians. Others said that they were not a Christian, and then, he instead shot them in the leg. They could have easily denied that they were a Christian, but so many people stood up and confessed who they were.

If you are assured that Christ is part of your life and that he's got plans and his will for your life and a way for you to live your life, then you will have confidence. You can share that confidence with others in these hard times. When scary topics, such as Syrian refugees and conflict and danger with terrorist attacks come up, you can share your peace with people. You can share that you're confident about where you are going after death, and you have peace in this world. You don't have to have your head in the sand; people are looking for a voice of reason at this time. They are not looking for others that just ignore the situation or that just pretend the situation isn't happening. They are looking to engage with people and to find answers. You can share with the community by being a light and by being available to share truth, wisdom and the knowledge of God and his ways and reasoning.

Now, we're going to get into some practical matters.

Encouraging Others

We live in a world where life can be pretty tough. People work many hours just to earn a living, and they might not even approach paying all the bills and credit cards. They have worries and concerns. They live in a world where so many advertisements are bombarding them, and the media makes it seem as if a person has to own a lot of material possessions to have a successful life. The average person faces a lot of pressure to survive and to get by. People are working in jobs and living their lives, doing the best they can. People are not doing sub-par or sub-standard work. And the world can be tough!

In this world, women look at how other women dress — they look at fashion and understand it as they see smart dresses, trendy skirts, fashionable tops and all sorts of desirable clothes on other women. Some women have more money and can afford better brands and fashions while some women are frugal and know how to shop at community shops or thrift stores where they buy quality clothes for inexpensive prices, still dressing themselves well. Some women really present themselves well, and they know what clothes and colors will accentuate their looks. Other women struggle to look good.

Let's look at one of these women who is struggling to look good. One day, she buys a dress but keeps it in her closet for six months just because she is not really confident enough to wear it. Some women need other people's encouragement before they can be happy with a piece of clothing. If she wears the dress to work one day, and you see her, you might compliment her and say, "Gee, that's a beautiful dress. That looks really good on you! How long have you had that? I haven't seen that before."

She might say, "I bought it a while ago. So you think that it looks good on me?"

"Oh yeah! It really brings out your eyes."

That compliment by you is really sweet to her ears. Of course, if a couple of people comment, then that dress will come out every two weeks. The lady is now confident and happy with her purchase.

You really helped make that dress a winner. Your comment and your love made her day and gave her a dress to rotate for work. Encouraging others is just a simple and easy thing to do. It even makes you feel good.

Of course, people might use encouragement and flattery as a way to control people. Many women have a hard time accepting a compliment from a man because many times, a man is trying to use it as leverage to develop some sort of rapport or even control over the woman. Women are very perceptive to this type of flattery and sometimes, even other women use flattery to gain control and position.

But we're not looking at that. We are looking at encouraging others. Most of the time, when you're genuine with your compliment, when you've got a good heart, and when you're coming from a generous spirit, people are able to recognize a compliment and accept it gratefully. Some people struggle with being encouraged, but it still touches them. Even though they don't acknowledge your compliment or say thank you and make a big fuss about what you've said, your words still encourage them and really brighten their day.

If you're known as a person who encourages people, then people like to be around you. People are never sure when something will come out of your mouth that's encouraging, but they love interacting with you.

Encouragement takes close observation. You have to be very observant to be a good encourager. As a supervisor on the job, you have to know which employees are doing an exceptional job. Her phone manner, her skill, her temperament, her self-control and her ability to control her patience is above average. You've got to be able to recognize all those things in the person taking the call. When you're the supervisor, and you walk by her between calls, you might pay her a compliment. You might tell her, "You're a patient person. You handled the customer really well. You had tremendous self-control; I'm really proud of you!"

That's what makes your call center the best. People like you. You're able to effectively oversee others because you are very observant, and you know what great work looks like. To become a good encourager, you need to take an interest and have an understanding of what good is, what excellent is, what exceptional is. To be able to recognize that in a person and bring it out into the open and publicly say that to the person is the gift of encouragement.

Building Up People

This is similar to encouragement. Building up people can be done when they are weak and struggling. Building up people means coming alongside them and lifting them up. When someone is having a problem in their marriage, and they share with you about it, you might offer to babysit their children so that they can go out on a date night. You are building up and encouraging people. You can offer to be the person they can talk to and tell them that you can meet them for coffee outside of work to build them up and give them confidence. If they feel free to share their concerns with you, it will help them. You can listen to them and offer any suggestions from your own marriage and experience with your spouse and children. That's a way of building up people.

People want to know that you care about them. People want to know that you will be there for them. As you develop trust with them, you develop that ability to be the person they come to. Through your experience and through many conversations and much understanding on your part, you become a vital person in their life.

If I have issues that I want to deal with, I'll always go to a person who will listen to me. I'll go to a person who has proven that they listen to me without judging. Everyone wants a person who listens and who is very understanding and not judgmental. You might not necessarily go to them for advice because you might be smart enough to work out things for yourself. But you will likely accept advice from someone who's a compassionate listener without being judgmental. You'll be open to what they say.

For instance, a year ago I had a pastor who was a really good friend, and I really loved him. During the three years that he was my pastor, he's only given me advice twice. Both times, I've listened to his counsel. Usually, he didn't need to offer advice but just listened with compassion and understanding. People want you to listen and to understand them. They want you to offer help and assistance when they are having a hard time.

For instance, I knew a person who was $50 short on their rent. They didn't know what they would do, and I gave them the $50 just to help out. I believe that this person needed the $50 for rent money and that they didn't use it for drugs or alcohol. Many people who know me feel the influence and the love of Jesus on me, and they won't lie to me because they respect the Christ in me. They're honest.

Influencing your world for Christ doesn't just affect non-Christians. We're told to be salt and light to everybody. For people who might be struggling in the Christian church, being salt and light means that you help supply those needs and help out others, encouraging them and building them up. Building up people is the same for everybody no matter who they are — Christians, Hindus, Muslims or Jews.

Being a Positive Voice

This world we live in is corrupt and getting dark and scary, and it appears to be coming apart at the seams. I'm not sure when you are reading this book, but if you are reading it in 2016 or 2017, I'm sure that ISIS is still a threat. Even if you're reading this book after ISIS has been dealt with, I'm sure you can remember when ISIS was a threat. We need people in this world that are positive and who can bring light to the situation. They can bring a positive voice that's calming and a voice of restoration, peace, control and stability in the situations that we're in. We need to be a good influence on people who don't know Jesus. It helps if you have a positive attitude and can provide an optimistic spin on that situation so that you can give encouragement and so that others can see the situation in a positive light.

You can be a true help to others if you're a person who is always encouraging them and building up people and if you have something positive to say in the face of negativity. You can bring solutions and answers through critical thinking instead of blindly following what the media says. If you know how to express yourself with understanding, then you can influence others and help them. People will come to you with their problems and concerns and ask for your opinion and input.

Many people start blogs and become an expert on a certain topic. Others follow those blogs, reading them every week. They enjoy taking 10 minutes to read the thoughts of an expert. If you are the positive voice in your workplace and if others can depend on you, they will be attracted to you. When you add in the other characteristics that we have covered so far, you become even more attractive. You don't have to be unrealistic to be positive. You don't have to smile all the time. You can express your fears and struggles with your feelings about letting refugees into your country.

On one hand, you understand having compassion so that people have a safe place to live out of harm's way. On the other hand, you do not want to let a Trojan horse into your nation.

So it's quite alright to express both sides. You can say that you want to show compassion but admit that you're also worried. Even so, you can be a positive influence and voice in the midst of that. People are interested in leaders and are attracted to someone influential that they can respect.

People often share posts on Facebook, and some of these have numerous shares. I saw a post just yesterday with 23 likes and 25 shares. In that instance, more people shared it than liked it. I think the 25 shares just pressed share without even liking it. Someone said something so powerful that they had to share it with their friends. People said to themselves, "I'm going to tell my friends what this leader said because I liked it so much."

This can happen with both positive and negative posts. Someone might post something that's such a worry and concern and people might share that. People are looking for leadership — for someone to stand apart and be a change and make a difference. While people want solutions to these topics, you might not have to share the answer. People are looking for others who think for themselves and who don't just blindly follow what the media says. They are looking for people with solid reasoning but who still have a positive attitude about it.

I can admit that if we had refugees come to Australia that I'd like checks done on them. If they can't be properly vetted, perhaps we shouldn't admit them. I'm not sure what the answer is; it's okay for me to share that I'm not sure of the solution! I certainly do not want terrorist attacks to start to break out in every country that accepts refugees. It's okay to share the conflicting feelings that I have on this topic. I'm sure that you aren't judging me for being honest with my thoughts.

You don't have to gloss over my opinion by saying that God is in control. People sometimes glibly say that God's controlling everything, so we'll just trust him. However, it's a misconception that God is in control. He's allowed us to have free will and allowed people to make their own decisions. As a result, evil sometimes happens due to the choices that evil people make. God really can't stop terrorist attacks. However, we can pray against them, and we can pray for wisdom, strength, knowledge and understanding when it comes to the security of our nation. Express how you feel, but remember that people are looking for you to be positive — they are looking for you to be salt, light and an encouragement and looking for those who will build up others. People are attracted to you as you offer the following: a listening ear, a voice of reason and a positive attitude. People will seek you out and ask your opinion, which is how you create influence in people's lives.

Bringing Joy to Others

Be someone who brings joy, laughter and fun to people's lives. You might not be a natural comedian or demonstrate a great sense of humor all the time, but you can still bring joy to the lives of others. Most people have a sense of humor, which helps lighten the burdens of life and releases endorphins. People really enjoy being around others with a sense of humor. Not everyone can be this way; people have different temperaments. You can make a difference by being yourself, being totally happy to be who you are, being able to share the trouble or struggles you're going through, being transparent and honest and encouraging people and building them up. If you can do all of this, you can become a joy bringer.

Before I received healing, even in the midst of chronic depression, I could go into an environment and bring joy. I'm like a comedian. Many of our comedians suffer from depression, yet through their lives and as they interact with situations, they see a potentially funny perspective. They might write a comedy skit and share something that's happened to them that was really funny. Underneath, they might be really depressed. But when they're in public or when they go on stage, they make everyone laugh for half an hour. They are joy bringers. Everyone loves a comedian and buys their DVDs or watches them on comedy shows. However, they might not know the comedian's personal life and struggles. They might not see the depressed part of him. Robin Williams was a great example of someone who struggled with depression his whole life but brought much joy to others through his comedy and his movies. My pastor approached me at church last year and said that he really enjoys how I encourage people. He really appreciates me and the inspiration that I am to others. He told me, "Even in the midst of your depression, you can encourage people. I'm really happy and impressed with how you encourage everyone else and bring so much life to our community even though you're not healed of your depression, Matthew!"

I was really happy and encouraged by his words. In the same way, you can bring joy to people. Read joke books and find the jokes and stories that are funny and that impress you and make you laugh. They are the best ones to share, and you can just ignore the ones that are not funny to you. You might even find jokes on Facebook in groups. Memorize the jokes and then, tell them whenever you have the opportunity to do so. Just be that person that tells jokes or stories that crack people up. The best jokes are the ones that make you laugh whenever you share them.

You can be that person who brings joy. If you have had a hard life, this has an even greater effect on people. You provide them with inspiration when they know that your personal life is a struggle. If you can do it, you will encourage others. Be a joy bringer. Look up some jokes if you need to and then share them with people. If you're naturally funny, just be yourself. Just bring joy to people.

Much of being a joy bringer is encouraging people. Be aware, be sensitive, look out for opportunities, look out for the good in people and compliment them. Tell them sincerely what a great job they are doing; tell them sincerely that their dress or jeans or make up looks really nice. Look for ways that you can compliment people. Once you open your eyes, you will be amazed at what you notice around you and at how easy it is to compliment others.

What affect do you have on people? Being encouraging does not mean that you are fake or that you are controlling people. Instead, you are being a positive influence. You are bringing life — bringing joy to the lives of others. Become that person. Reinvent yourself if you need to so that you are an encourager.

You might read through this section and think that you are not a funny person or a great encourager. This gift might not come naturally to you. Don't worry as we have a number of subjects to cover. You might do better with some of the others. Focus on those instead.

Since I first recorded this, I have received deliverance and for five months, I have not struggled with depression. I am happy that I am no longer suffering and that my personal life is different. Even so, I am still the joy bringer.

Not Speaking Ill of People

So many people in this world, in the church and outside of the church gossip or speak ill of others. So many! It's like a favorite pastime. I think they enjoy gossiping so much because it makes them feel better and even superior to the person they are talking about and putting down. This is an example:

"Do you know what Betty did? She asked Bob out and practically seduced him. And you know that Bob is happily married. So Betty overlooked him for the promotion and said that the promotion is conditional on the sex. What a *****!"

You can set yourself apart when people are gossiping by bringing up good points about the person. You might say, "Betty has led a troubled life, and I can understand why she thinks that sex is a way to gain control. You should see her art work. Have you ever been to her house and seen her paintings? She is an amazing artist! She might have some personal problems — and who among us doesn't? — but she is talented. I think that she could earn a living just from her art work."

Just by casually dropping that into the conversation and by being a master at doing it, you can change atmospheres. When people are gossiping, turn the conversation to something positive by saying something kind, such as, "Have you ever seen her doodles? She doodles and draws when she is answering phones. They are amazing! You should see them! Ask her if you can have a look at her pad the next time you walk by her desk. You know, you might even find a picture of yourself — she drew one of me. It was really outstanding!"

Try to change how you respond. You don't have to tell people that you don't want to gossip or that you don't want any part of their conversation. That takes effort because the world is made up of people whose favorite thing to do is gossip. But you can be different and stand out. Every time people start to speak ill of someone, you can speak well about the person.

You can be among people that gossip without joining in the conversation and speaking ill of people. So many people in this world are hurt and are hurting. So many people need deliverance and counseling. So many people have had a past that really hurt them, and they haven't recovered from it. Gossip is like putting a Band-Aid on your skin when someone shot you with a gun. People gossip to feel good about themselves and to make themselves look better than the person they are gossiping about. They think they are boosting themselves up. Instead, just like that Band-Aid, they are ineffectively trying to cover up the hurt that's inside them.

It's similar to social media arguments when you watch two or three people go back and forth on a Facebook thread. People love to watch the arguments and fights and even violence. They love picking on each other, and some people will even join in to add to the argument and add fire to the confrontation. It's good to be a peacemaker.

If you repeatedly followed these suggestions in your workplace, you would have a powerful impact. You could change the behavior of your work associates if you changed the subject during gossip and instead made positive statements about the person. They would simply stop gossiping whenever you turned up as they would clearly know that you don't participate in that. And you know, if they had problems and if people were gossiping about them or if they were depressed and losing friends, they would come to you because they would know that you weren't listening to gossip about them. They would know that you would have positive things to say about them.

You can make a real difference once you decide to do it. It's easy to do — at least for me. Most of what I am writing about are things I already do, and I am sharing the lessons that I have already learned and what I have put into practice with you, the reader.

Sharing Your Struggles with People

You can be an effective witness to people and stand out as totally different from many Christians by being open and sharing your struggles with them. This takes effort and a willing decision to be vulnerable. Some people think that being a Christian means that you don't have any problems or struggles. They think that being an effective witness to others means hiding their troubles when they have difficulties. This shouldn't be true when you are witnessing to non-Christians. However, this can be the case in many churches. People sometimes wear masks when they come to church and act like everything is fine. They pretend that they aren't having any trouble or suffering in their lives.

You might find out too late that:

A person has lost their job

A marriage has broken down

A child has become addicted to drugs or

They haven't been able to pay their mortgage.

These are just some of the things that can happen to people in churches all around the world. People come to church every week and share that everything is fine and dandy. Tragic events happen to them, and you wonder what went wrong because they told you a week ago that everything was fine. Christians live this shallow life without being vulnerable and open with others. If you are living this way, I pray that you will learn how to open up to your church family.

Many Christians feel even more compelled to hide their life from non-Christians. They somehow mistakenly think that not sharing their sufferings with other people is going to be a better witness to non-Christians. In fact, the opposite is true. When you share your struggles with non-Christians, you build rapport with them. When you are transparent with people and when they watch you struggle, they are able to see Christ and the hope and glory that is within you. They can see your attitude and how you navigate through the problems in your life.

If you're divorced, you might share that you've had trouble seeing your children. Your former spouse might be stopping you from visiting them. Sharing that struggle with people allows them to see that you are human and that you go through the same problems that everyone else does. Through this, they come to realize that being a Christian doesn't mean that you don't have problems. The Christian life doesn't have to be a life of perfection or a life where everything goes perfectly.

They see that just because you have Jesus in your life doesn't mean that you don't have the normal day-to-day struggles that others have. This provides an amazing opportunity for you to share and witness to people when you share your problems with them. People who care for you are interested in you. People mistakenly think that a non-Christian wouldn't be interested in hearing about their difficulties, but the opposite is actually true.

Part of what makes an interesting television show or movie is the opposition that the characters face as the show progresses. The hardship and the villains in the movie that are in conflict with the lead character give the whole movie flavor. A movie wouldn't be a movie without some sort of struggle. Jesus is just as much a part of person's life whether they are doing well or struggling.

People need to understand that a normal Christian life isn't free of troubles or trying circumstances. Instead, the normal Christian life is your ability to handle these tragedies and trials that you go through. Being authentic and real and sharing your struggles is an effective way to witness to people and share your life with them. People don't want to see a candy-coated picture or a façade that looks great on the outside but that is full of wickedness and trouble and disaster on the inside. People don't want to see white-washed tombs as Jesus called them. He wants you to be real and authentic with people. The more that you are real and authentic with people, the more you will be understood and listened to by the people that you're ministering to.

Being Transparent

Being transparent is the ability to share honestly what you're going through, what you have been through and what you are thinking. People want to understand how you're thinking, and they want to know your decisions and your thought processes. They want to know how you're going to react. People who are friends of yours, who you're interacting with, want to know that you are a person with real struggles and hardships. They want to know how you're dealing with them.

You can hide and deal with your problems silently, and you can live a life like many Christians do. You can keep your troubles from others and think that you're more "righteous" and holy by doing so. However, when you share your struggles and trials with others, when you are transparent with them, you really manage to shine the light of Christ in other people's lives. I have found that sharing parts of my life and my struggles in various books that I've written really tends to draw people closer to me. They open up with me, which draws them into my life and my experiences. Sharing things honestly shows people that I'm a real person who is dependable and that what I say is trustworthy. They don't view me as just someone with no experience who writes a book or who only focuses on information and who doesn't share personal matters about his life to illustrate points.

I like to illustrate points that I make by being transparent. For example, when I talked about not being able to see your child because your spouse didn't allow it, I was speaking about my own life. I went through 16 years without access to my son. When my former wife remarried, she told me that I would not be able to see my son anymore. When I fought a custody battle for the right to have access to him, I suffered an attack of witchcraft on my life and ended up in a psychiatric ward. I had a nervous breakdown due to the warfare that was involved. My former wife threatened me that if I fought her in court that I would end up back in the hospital again.

Another friend of mine met my wife, and she told me that my former wife used witchcraft. This friend advised me not to see my son anymore, so I took her counsel. Jesus told me to walk away from my son and leave him to the man that my former wife was marrying.

As a result, I spent 16 years with no communication with my boy. During those years, at Christmas and Easter holidays when people celebrate and get excited, I was really sad and depressed. Although I can email my son and have contact with him today, we're still not close. We don't have a great relationship, so I still have trouble during Christmas and Easter. I don't get into the festive mood like other people because of this breakdown in the relationship with my son.

When people know that you're been through this type of suffering and that you've come out strong on the other end, they feel encouraged. When you share these types of stories, people feel that you can be trusted with their troubles. Amazingly, many fathers have had their relationship break down with their wife and haven't been able to see their children. As you share sad stories, people have the opportunity to relate similar stories and troubles. They feel that you're approachable and that you're a person who would understand them because you've shared so openly about your life.

Although the analogy might be odd, I feel that I'm supposed to share this. It's like a mouse trap. When you are transparent and talk about your problems, it's like you're putting a bit of cheese on the mouse trap. You're putting bait out there for other people to sample who don't know Christ. Sharing your struggles is like the bait. It might take months or even years, but some of those people end up approaching you with their own burdens and asking you questions and for advice about certain situations that they find themselves in simply because you've been transparent with them. You've been willing to share your life with them, so they feel comfortable and at ease with you. As a result, they open up, and you can share quite honestly that you have a relationship with Jesus Christ, and he carries you through all your trials and helps you cope. You can talk about your faith in him.

The person might already know that you are a Christian, so you can share your beliefs at the appropriate time. In any case, when you are transparent with people, it allows them to understand you and to feel comfortable with you.

I hope that through my story, you understood that I am very much aware of the spirit of witchcraft. Many Christians have the Jezebel spirit, which is a type of witchcraft that can come against you. In the past week, since I recorded the first video for this book, I came under tremendous attack and fell into quite a deep depression. When the depression became too much, I posted on Facebook with a trusted group of friends that I needed prayer and about 30 people prayed for me to come out of that depression.

During that week, while I battled with depression, I couldn't work on the rest of the book. I just couldn't get myself into the mood to make a video and share. Targeted witchcraft over my life caused me to fall into a depression where I couldn't move forward with the project that I have to record this book on video and have it transcribed. Witchcraft, through the Jezebel spirit, can affect you in a very discernable way and can make a real impact on your life. That's the spirit my former wife had, and she was operating in a type of witchcraft when I had the court battle that ended up with me going to the hospital.

This scary spirit really affects people. I don't normally feel sad and get discouraged. I am not usually distracted from making videos and working on the next portion of my book. This was an actual attack on my life by a person with a Jezebel spirit. Like I said before, I ended up in deep depression, which caused me to be unable to get in the right spirit and the right mood to record the second part of this video series for the book.

For some of you who have been attacked by that same spirit, my experience brings comfort and more revelation to you. If you haven't been attacked by that spirit, you can receive more personal understanding so that you can be better prepared.

I use stories and illustrations when I speak and through my books to demonstrate a point and emphasize it. When you're transparent, nothing is off limits for you to share. You can share anything, and you have the ability to open up about different subjects with people and discuss things that are really close to your heart with them. You will find that people really appreciate honesty, and they really appreciate someone who is transparent. They feel quite a bit closer to a person who will open up and share their struggles and their life. As such, vulnerability is a key to open up the hearts of people.

Influencing Your World FOR Christ

As I have shared before, it's been five months since I have had deliverance, and I have not succumbed to full-blown depression since then. I praise God that he has healed me again. It is risky to be honest and transparent with people, but I can assure you that it opens doors of opportunity to people's hearts.

Sharing Your Faith in Normal Conversations

It is a particularly good habit if you can share about Jesus and your faith in normal conversation. The other day, I was at a meeting for Toastmasters, which is a public speaking group. Someone shared with me over a drink that he has a roommate with amazing authority. When he speaks, he just impresses the whole room. The whole room goes silent, and everyone is in awe of what he says. I shared with him that one time, Jesus preached and shared through me for two hours. If Jesus paused for 10 seconds, I panicked and wondered whether he was going to keep on sharing because his words were awesome. He had so much authority in what he was saying, and it was so inspiring and the most amazing message I have ever heard in my life. I told him, "That might be hard for you to understand as you don't normally hear these types of stories."

He agreed with me and understood why I shared it. While that might be an extreme case of sharing your faith with other people, this person took two things away from our conversation. He understands that I have faith in Jesus and that I hear from him so that Jesus can speak through me. He might ponder about these two subjects as he walks away, but he will certainly remember these two things about our meeting.

You don't have to lead people in a sinner's prayer the first time or even the first month that you meet them. But whenever you have the opportunity to share a story about your faith, you can come to a place where you are comfortable sharing about Jesus. If Jesus is a big part of your life and has made an impact on you, then it's as easy as sharing a story with people of when you went to the grocery store the last time. When you arrived, you found a special on a certain item that you were looking for and how wonderful it was. You can share in the story that you were $5 short because you knew the prices of what you had to buy, and you didn't have enough money. However, when you went down to the shop, God amazingly had arranged for three of the products you needed to be on sale, so you actually had just enough money to cover your purchase.

You can share the story in one of two ways. You can share that you were short $5, and then the items were on special, or you can share that God was a part of it and that he arranged for the products to be cheaper. You have a personal choice about how much you talk about God when it comes to many stories that you share. Of course, you should include Jesus or God in the stories you share. Even so, you don't have to go overboard. You don't want people to think that you are overly religious or that you're always preaching to them. However, you certainly don't have to hold back when you talk about your faith.

Many people feel that non-Christians have no interest in hearing about Jesus and God and hearing stories that involve them. If you're living a life that's close to Jesus, you have many testimonies of how Jesus has interacted with and impacted you. Just share your faith with people in stories that you tell and as a natural part of the conversations that you have with people. Help people understand that Jesus is very real to you; he didn't die 2,000 years ago and stayed buried. Instead, he is an active part of your life; he is someone that you believe in and know, and you interact with him every day of your life. People want to know that he is real because as they have questions about faith and as they go through struggles, they want to be impacted by the same Jesus that you know. When you share stories with many people about how Jesus changed your life, they might not say much to you, but they might go away wishing that Jesus would touch them like he touched you. Not everyone will express that they want the same relationship with Jesus, but it doesn't mean that they don't.

You have choices when you share your testimony. Like I said before about the shopping and the specials, you can tell the same story to a person without using God or Jesus, or you can share the story using God and Jesus and give them the glory. And that's just a simple story. However, when I shared with the person that Jesus spoke through me for two hours, I could not share that story without explaining that Jesus was the one speaking through me. I didn't share that story to convert the person, but I was just illustrating a point that similar to his roommate, Jesus speaks with a lot of authority.

When Jesus speaks through me, I've heard myself speaking with this type of authority under the inspiration of the Holy Spirit. I took advantage of the opportunity. Now, I could have chosen not to use that open door to speak. I could be speaking to a person, and the idea of that illustration could come to my mind, and I could choose right then not to share it. The choice is up to me, just as Jesus doesn't force you to witness and evangelize people. Not only does he not force you to talk about him with others, but he doesn't want anyone else to force you to evangelize, either. Witnessing and sharing your faith should always be a choice, which I am free to make.

I had a conversation with another person from Toastmasters. He thinks most churches have been mismanaged because of pedophilia that has been uncovered in many of the churches in Australia where I live. At the time, the royal inquiry into pedophilia was being reported on TV, and no Christian organizations have been exempt from the inquiries. He is disgusted with the Christian faith and thinks the whole Christian faith is not run well because these people have been allowed to abuse children. I shared with him that pedophiles will choose an organization and specific places where they can influence children so that they have the opportunity to abuse kids.

I told him that it's not so much the organization, but it's the predators and pedophiles who find places in organizations where they can abuse children. He accepted my point that it happens in every organization that involves children, not just Christian ones. Even so, I said that doesn't excuse the organizations. The organizations should screen people better and not allow pedophiles to be a part of their staff. They should have excellent vetting in place so that pedophiles don't have this opportunity. I didn't win the argument, but I had a meaningful conversation with that man.

After a year, this man and I have grown pretty close. I had the chance to prophesy over him and the group of people that come for drinks after the meeting once, and now, this man often asks me for a prophecy over him and other people. I can demonstrate Christ and the Christian faith to this guy. Through my speeches of six to eight minutes, I can share with him and others about my faith and what I've learned as a Christian. Through our connection in Toastmasters, I can impact him through personal conversations over the coming months and years. You need to learn to share your faith with people and to include your Christian faith in normal conversations.

Actively Listening to People

Many people have the habit of actively thinking about how they will respond during a conversation while the other person is speaking. This isn't love. It is not what God requires of us or how he wants us to act. He wants us to learn how to listen to others and to really hear what people say rather than just waiting until it's our turn to talk. He wants us to take the time and effort to listen to a person and to what they are saying and then ask them questions about their thoughts to open the door for a deeper discussion. God would love for you to think of questions that will further develop the course of the conversation and that will dig deeper into the topic that the person is talking about. Keep asking them questions about the subject they're discussing. Asking questions shows them that you're really interested in what they have to say.

Most people really like to talk about themselves and share their lives with others. If you can be one of those people that spends time listening to others, and if you can be a person who always has a listening ear for them, then you become someone who is special in that person's life. They know that when they see you that they can speak to you and that you'll be there for them and that you'll listen to them. If you'll listen to their concerns and listen to what they have to say, then you will become important to them.

Life is busy, including people participating on social media and posting on Facebook. People might sit on trains these days and search Facebook and respond to comments without even talking to those around them. You can interact with people on Facebook by actually liking someone's post, which makes a person feel appreciated. For example, certain people seem to like everything I say, which really means something to me. Liking a person's post is a form of listening to them; it's saying I've heard what you say, and I like your thoughts.

Another way to interact with a person and make them know that they've been heard is to take the actual time and make the effort to comment on their post. This demonstrates a higher level of engagement with them.

When people are talking with you face to face, really listen to what the person is saying rather than having your mind distracted and thinking about other things. Show them love by fully engaging with them and giving them your full attention to show them that you're interested in them. You don't have to always be thinking, "When am I going to have the opportunity to share Christ and what he's done in my life with this person?" You don't have to have an agenda for a person as you share life together.

I feel that I should advise you to simply listen to people in such a way that you can ask questions and respond to what they are saying. This will help really open them up. As they speak about each facet of their life and the related topics, think of things that you can ask. Keep that in mind as they continue speaking and then, when there's a break, ask the question that relates to what they just have been saying and listen to them again. You can have an amazing effect on a person when you truly listen to people.

Some people are busy apologizing to me for speaking so much when the conversation ends. Often people say to me that I'm a really good person to have a conversation with, and sometimes, we haven't really had much of a two-way conversation. Sometimes, I've just been listening to a person for half an hour.

Jesus invests his time into us. So many times, we pray to Jesus and talk to him, and he just listens and listens and listens to us. He is so responsive and so loving that he'll just listen to us. He will watch us all day and see how we interact, and he'll just listen to us. In this way, listening to people is really important when building relationships. It's a vital thing to do with people and really encourages them to love and appreciate you for who you are.

Remember to Follow Up

When you see a person frequently, you should ask them a question or bring a subject up that they were talking about the last time that you were together. Even if you see a person every day, follow up with your previous conversation — playing sports, going to dinner with their wife or helping their child with homework. Next time you see them, ask about that topic.

This lets people know that you are both listening and really interested in their lives. You are investing your time in them. People want to feel that they are important and to know that their lives count for something. They want to be sure that others care about and appreciate them. And one way to show Christ is to be there for people and to listen to them and to engage them in conversations and discussions. Personally, I am really impressed when people hear me say something, and they follow up on the subject later.

For example, I once told my pastor's father that I was going home to record a book. Later on, he asked me if I actually recorded it like I said I would. That showed me that he was listening to what I had said and that he was interested in me and in what I was saying. It also showed that he wanted to see if I was a person of my word and if I did what I said I was going to do. I told him that I did record the videos for the book, "7 Keys to Intimacy with Jesus," which is actually a video series on my YouTube channel as well as a paperback and e-book available on Amazon. You can check out on my YouTube channel if you are interested in more of my material.

At the time, I told my pastor's father that I did record three videos that night. However, I was not happy with the recordings, so the next week, I deleted the videos and did another video recording of them.

He was interested and asked, "Is the book finished?"

I answered that it was and that it now had to be transcribed and edited. First, I edit it myself, and then, I have to pay someone to edit it further. After that, it will be ready to be made into a book. So in this situation, he showed that he cared about me and that he was listening to what I said weeks before. He wanted to know if I was a person of my word that followed through with what I said I would do, which showed his interest in me. His concern actually made me feel good about myself, which made me happy to be able to share the progress that I'd made with my book.

One aspect of following up is to listen to a person and ask questions about what they are talking about and help them elaborate on the subject more fully. Another aspect is that you can follow up on past conversations and show that you are interested in them beyond just talking to them every week. Show that you have an active interest in what they are saying and doing.

This pastor's father really impressed me and made me happy. I was really encouraged to share things with him. When someone listens to you and follows up with you and asks you questions about what you're going to do, it shows you that they love you and are interested in you. In turn, this encourages you to share more with them about what you've already discussed.

Your life will improve if you listen to what I'm telling you and if you take the time and make the effort to apply the advice in these pages.

Finally, do not have an agenda. Like I've already said, you shouldn't be thinking about when you will preach to the person or share the Gospel with him or her or if you will lead them to Christ. You shouldn't have conversations and interactions with people with that in mind. Instead, trust that the Holy Spirit knows how to work on a person's mind. Trust that he knows how to inspire the person to ask you questions about your faith. Trust that he will tell you and give you the opportunity to speak into a person's life regarding Jesus and your faith. The process of sharing shouldn't come as a jolt or be harsh or confrontational. It should flow easily and come naturally to you in a conversation.

Taking an Interest in Their Interests

While we're listening to people and engaging and interacting with them, you can make the effort to take an interest in what interests them. You might not be particularly into golf, so talking about golf might bore you. However, you can just consider that it is something that you need to do to actually take an interest in the person's sport. As they talk about golf, you might be aware that the Australian Open or the US Open was just played. Pay attention to when golf is on TV in the future so that you know which players are winning and which ones aren't doing well. Take an active interest in golfing news so that you can bring it up in conversations with your friend. They will likely be quite impressed that you don't play golf and are not a fanatic about the sport, but they will appreciate you sharing that you know who won the US Open or the Australian Open.

They will appreciate that you're taking the time and making the effort to talk to them about something that interests them. You know, I feel that Jesus is most impressed with people who don't only listen to him but who live their lives according to how he taught and live their lives according to the directions he gave. Some people say that they love Jesus and follow him. Jesus is their Savior, but Jesus isn't their Lord. They don't live by Jesus' commands and his directions as found in the Bible. Jesus is a loving person, but he is impressed by those who not only read and listen to what he says but those who actually do what he says. When you take an interest in a person, be it Jesus or be it a stranger or a co-worker, it makes an impression on them. When you start to talk about things that interest them and bring up conversations and remind them of what you have talked about and ask them about what they said they were going to do, this really shows a person that you've taken an interest in them, which really impresses people.

Once again, I have to repeat this often. Don't do this with an agenda to save a person. We're here to be the love of Christ. You know Jesus shared that we're to love God with all our mind, heart and soul, and we're to love others as we love ourselves. That's a commandment. Living according to the way of Jesus is how you show that you love others. These directions that I'm giving are all examples of the ways that you can practically live out that commandment to love other people as you love yourself. You love other people as they talk to you; you love other people when you listen to them; you love other people when you take an active interest in what interests them.

You love them as you share your heart with them and dialogue with them and are really interested in what they have to say. And because you love other people, they will love you in return.

Jesus said, "Do unto others as you would have them do unto you." That is the perfect response to someone in a situation about talking to others and interacting with them.

For example, I was talking to a friend at church, and I mentioned something that she'd told me months before. She was shocked as she said, "I'm surprised that you remember that!"

I replied, "I remember everything." She was really surprised and touched.

Later on, she said, "I really like you, Matthew! I really like talking to you." Of course, she is a Christian but showing love to a person, remembering what they say and taking interest in them is a wonderful thing to do. It makes a big impact on people and really touches their hearts. You don't know how your conversations and how taking an interest in someone will have an effect on a person.

You don't fully understand the stress that people are under. You don't know the pressures that are in their lives. Some people are facing challenges, and they aren't full of joy, and they deal with a lot of stress and troubles. Having someone that talks to them and that comes alongside them and shares their heart with them and takes an interest in them could be the only thing that keeps that person going. By demonstrating your concern, you could be the favorite person in someone else's life. You could be one of the reasons that they are still living and pressing on and going on.

How would you like to be that person to someone else? They might look forward to spending time with you each week. They might look forward to talking to you and sharing their heart with you. How would you like to be the person that someone at work singles out and decides to befriend? How would you like to be the reason a person is living and the reason that the person is motivated and happy with life, despite all of the pressures and the stress that they face? You can be that person to someone else.

Be a Friend without Expecting Anything in Return

People in this life want friends. They want others to love, appreciate, respect and encourage them. Yet many people miss out when they don't have the attitude that in order to win a friend, it's better to be a friend. Sadly, most people have this hierarchy as they have a certain type of person that they want to be friends with while they ignore other people.

Many people have hard lives and are suffering. They live on pensions, Social Security or government assistance. They are sad and depressed and struggle with addictions. These people truly need an upstanding, upright friend. They truly need someone in their life that is an example of solid values and integrity. They could really use an example — someone whose life is going very well and who is righteous and strong with qualities that the world respects in others. You could be that friend to many people — a place of refuge, a strong tower. You could be a person that attracts the broken hearted who run to you to share their hearts and lives.

Many of us are looking for people who are on the same level as us in prosperity and success. We have no interest in people that are suffering and going through a hard time. However, I would dare to say that these are the sort of people that God is calling us to — the broken hearted and the hurting.

A Scripture verse that is one of my life's themes says this plainly. I want to share it with you. Isaiah 42:6-7

"I, the Lord, have called you in righteousness, And I will hold your hand; I will keep You and give you as a covenant to the people, As a light to the Gentiles, To open blind eyes, To bring out prisoners from prison, Those who sit in darkness from the prison house."

The Lord has called us to open the eyes of people who are blind to Jesus. He is calling us to people who can't see Jesus and who are not aware of him. He is calling us to those people to help them see Jesus for who he is, to help them to see the reality of Jesus and the fact that Jesus loves them. Some of these people don't have a Bible, and they aren't open to hearing from Jesus. For those people, we're the only Jesus they will meet. We need to be that Jesus and that example for people. We need to reach out and touch them. We need to bring prisoners out of prison. To do that, we have to go and visit the prison ourselves. You can't bring the prisoner out of prison if you won't visit the prison.

This is an example of God speaking to us. He is saying to go where people are sitting in darkness and are afflicted and are in bondage. You need to open the prison doors and help release people so that they can come out from the prison house and be set free. For some people, it might take months while others might take years before they actually ask you a question so that you can share about Jesus.

I knew a person, a gay male, who worked at a video or DVD store. When I learned that he was a gay, I had my Bible with me. He told me, "You people don't like us people."

I replied, "I assume you mean that since I have a Bible, that I'm a Christian. And I assume you mean that Christians don't like people who are gay. I've never asked you if you're gay before. But that's what I assume."

He said, "That's right!"

I said, "Let my example and my friendship speak to you as to whether I love you or not and whether I care for you or not. Now that I know you're a gay, pay attention to how I treat you in the coming years and let that answer your question as to whether Christians love gays."

I really feel that answer was given to me by the Holy Spirit because it was such a wise answer.

Well, about five years later, he came to me, and he asked me to pray for him.

I asked, "What is it about?"

He said, "I need to move to another apartment, and I need roommates to be able to afford the new place. I'm having a hard time, and I've got to move out in two weeks. I don't have much time left. Can you pray for me?"

He was acknowledging that I serve the real God who could fix his problems if I prayed. He recognized that the God that I serve is real, and he assumed that I had authority and the power to pray a prayer that would affect his life. A week later, he thanked me for praying for him, and he said that he found the apartment with new roommates.

About a year later, I was talking to him and the subject of angels came up. He asked me if he had an angel.

I said, "Yeah. You've got a female angel."

He asked, "What's her name?"

I answered, "Her name is Priscilla."

There was a famous movie made by Australians called "Priscilla Queen of the Desert" about gay people, so he really loved the idea that his angel's name was Priscilla.

I said, "Do want to hear from her?"

He said, "I'd love to."

I told him, "I'm going to tell that angel of yours to give you a message from God for me."

So I prayed. Then, I instructed him, "Now say what comes to your mind."

He then repeated what the angel said to him about me.

Then he said, "I feel chills; I feel like joy and love; it's amazing."

I told him, "That's what the presence of God feels like. That message for me was your angel speaking to you."

He exclaimed, "This is really cool."

I had that effect on him while I knew him. The video store closed shortly after that. But I prayed with him one other time, and he had another encounter with his angel. He knows that the angel was real, and he had goose bumps and felt the peace and the joy of the presence of God on him. That's the fruit of my relationship with him. God is quite able to take the seeds that I have planted in his life and further minister to him and lead him to Christ.

Give Them Time

Many people need your time, even if you just listen to them for a half an hour to an hour. They don't need anything except for you to listen to them. We need to give our time to others.

If a person needs help moving, they really appreciate it if you offer your time and energy. If they need a babysitter or meals cooked for them or chores done around the house to make a difference, you can be that person that spends time ministering to others. We have to remember not to have an agenda with people. We have to realize that some of the people that we spend time with will go on to become Christians in time and be converted by our example.

Some of the people might not become converted and become Christians while we know them. Even so, we can't treat everyone according to how we think things will play out. We just need to be Jesus to people and have no agenda when it comes to others. Instead, just spend time with people who need you without any agenda or trying to change them.

We should not judge them according to where we think they are on the spectrum of coming to Jesus or not. We should treat everyone equally and be loving. When Jesus was on earth, he spent time with all sorts of people — the prostitutes, the sinners, the publicans and the tax collectors. He spent time with the people who really needed him the most.

He also spent time with the Pharisees and teachers of the law, but he had to do that so that they could determine if he was the Messiah or not. The Pharisees spent time with anyone who claimed to be the Messiah. He was usually nice to them and gave them his time so that he could obey what his Father was saying. Even so, the Pharisees criticized him for spending his time with the broken-hearted. Likewise, that's what we're called to do.

Of course, we're called to spend time with people who have jobs and who are in the upper echelons of society. We're called to the whole spectrum of people that we do life with. We're not just called to the broken hearted and the hurting, but it's important for us to make sure that we allocate our time when it's needed. Some people have many needs, and they are really suffering and lonely with no friends. We don't want to distance ourselves from these sorts of people. Instead, we should continue to have productive interactions with them.

❧ ❖ ☙

Friendship with no Agenda but to Be Jesus to Them

I briefly covered this in a previous section. It's very important to be Jesus to people, to be salt — one that preserves flavor — and to be light — to demonstrate the light of Jesus Christ to people. We should not have a set agenda. I think many people who are not saved are upset with Christians because Christians approach them with an agenda. They think that the only reason the Christian wants to spend time with them is because the Christian has an agenda of "saving" them and of leading them to Christ.

For instance, I know people on the internet. They contact me and ask for a prophetic word. They go through the niceties of asking how I am. But eventually, they ask something similar to this: "Is God saying anything to you for me? Has God put anything on your heart?" It really frustrates me when people only come to me to hear from God. They are abusing my prophetic office. It really upsets me that people seem to have an agenda regarding their friendship with me. They seem to have this agenda to hear from God through me. It frustrates me to know that the only reason they have become my friend is because they know I am a prophet, so they want to approach me for a prophetic word.

In a similar way, non-Christians sense it when you have an agenda with them. They might intuitively pick up on the fact that you're only being friendly to them so that you can convert them to Christianity. This will cause a barrier from the beginning of your relationship. They won't be as receptive. We need to keep this in mind. We have to learn to just demonstrate Jesus to people and be relaxed about it.

Please hear me. I'm not saying that you can't share Jesus and the Gospel with people. I'm not saying that you can't give them books about Jesus or Christianity that will lead them closer to Jesus. I'm just saying don't have an agenda when it comes to people. Just be Jesus, just be love and just love people and who they are. Don't put a time frame on how long it will take to minister to them. You will know when God tells you to move on to someone else. Let him decide.

We've no idea when our love will ever bear fruit. It took years for my gay friend at the video store to ask me for prayer when he needed to move. Later, my influence in his life allowed him to ask about whether he had angels or not. First, I built up a relationship with him over the years. Remember that when he first saw me with a Bible, he announced, "You people don't like people like us." He would have shut me down completely if I had started to preach to him right away and to tell him that he can't be gay and practice homosexuality or he is going to go hell. I might have been telling him the truth, but my method wouldn't be effective.

We need to love people for who they are without a particular agenda. Even the agenda of eventually winning them to Christ is a wrong agenda. When I speak of this, I can't help but think of my former pastor, Mitchell. He just loves people and is an example of love. He spends time with them and pours love into people's lives. Like the rest of us, he's busy with only a certain amount of hours in each day. He has a lot of paper work to do and other obligations at his office at our community center. Still, he does come out to spend time with people and interact with them. He was always available to me whenever I went there and talked about things on my heart and what I was going through.

No matter why I was there — if I was struggling with sin, feeling guilty or had something on my mind — he was there for me. He let me know that I was loved and that Jesus loved me. He demonstrated the fact that Jesus loved me by how he loved and accepted me.

Buying this book is a good way to learn how to influence your world for Christ, but we don't have to be overzealous about it. We don't have to be intense and overbearing, but we can be just as effective simply by treating people with love and respect.

Support During Times of Trouble

You might not know how to reassure people that you're going to be there for them when they have problems. You likely can't specifically tell someone, "Hey, if you're ever in trouble, I'm going to be in your corner."

You might never overtly say that to a person, but they might know it through your relationship with them. When you demonstrate love to a person, they have a sense that you'll be there for them in times of trouble. Trouble comes up in many people's lives, and these people have you to turn to when they need help. They might lose their jobs, and you can demonstrate that you're not just friends while you're co-workers. You can still be friends when they are unemployed or have a different job. You can meet outside work at a coffee shop and continue your friendship.

My sister has known people who are not Christians for years. She does life with them through their ups and downs. She is a true friend to them. Australia has a course called "Christianity Explained," a six-week study that people go through to help them understand the Gospel of Jesus Christ. After about eight to 10 years of being friends with two non-Christian families, my sister invited them to take this course. She told them that she just wanted to share with them what Christianity actually means during the six weeks.

Because she had sown so much time into them, during good times and bad, and because she'd been there for them, these people were open to it and curious to know about her faith. The parents and the children in these families really loved her. She was one of their favorite friends. She had the two families meet for six nights over six weeks, and she explained her faith to them and invited them to make a decision for Christ. Ten people attended the course, and 9 of the 10 gave their lives to Jesus Christ. About four weeks later, the tenth person also made a commitment to Jesus.

You can find out more about that course here http://www.christianityexplained.com.

Now, when did they actually come to Christ? Was it during that six-week period, or did they come to Christ over the 10 years that my sister was a friend of these people? She earned the privilege of being able to share the Gospel with them, but she took 10 years before she approached them about it. She had a fully developed relationship with them.

The best way to win the confidence of a person is to be there when they have struggles. Your decision to stand up for them means a lot. Depending on the situation, that will look different. It might even mean that you stand up for them and speak out when they are coming under pressure in the workplace or when people are gossiping about them. They will appreciate your example. It might relate to their marriage, an addiction, financial matters or other struggles. We can support them and be with them in many ways during these rough patches.

Actively Help when Difficulties Come

We have touched on this topic a bit, but it's very important to be a friend in good times and bad. Some friends are only around when it's sunshine and when things are going well. But these sorts of friends aren't around when troubles hit. We have all known of friendships when people disappear when calamities strike.

Many of us know the parable of the Prodigal Son and how he had many friends in society when he lived it up and partied and slept with prostitutes. However, when the money ran out, all his supposed friends left. We don't need to be a friend like that. Our example and demonstration of Christ to people will seriously be affected if we betray others when they have struggles or times of difficulties. You should choose to be a friend in the good times and the bad. You should carry through that example of friendship, which is important to Jesus.

Jesus doesn't let go of us when we struggle. When we go through difficulties in our faith, he stays with us. In fact, he is often closer to us in those times, and we feel closer to him and feel a more intimate relationship during those hard times. Jesus connects with us more intimately during our struggles, so we should follow his example when it comes to dealing with others.

Learn how to Lead a Person to Christ

We should realize that we might not be the one that leads a person to Christ. We might not have my sister's experience with the 10 people. The Holy Spirit is very smart. As Christians, we don't really understand his role and how he speaks to people and gives non-Christians messages. The Holy Spirit and angels can direct non-Christians. Satan isn't the only one who can speak to their minds. The Holy Spirit can lead their thoughts and lead them in the direction that they need to go. We need to be assured that as long as we're praying for people and demonstrating love to them, the Holy Spirit knows what he is doing when it comes to peoples' lives. He knows how to witness to them, how to demonstrate Christ to them, how to speak to them and how to lead them.

When we think that everything is up to us, we fall into self-righteousness and pride on one extreme or guilt and condemnation on the other extreme if we feel that we aren't doing enough. When we focus on ourselves and not on God and his ways, we can be proud of what we are doing or upset and fearful about what we're not doing. Instead, he wants us to be happy with what we're doing without moving into self-righteousness and pride. We need to trust that when we're praying for people and living life with them and demonstrating Christ to them through our daily lives that the Holy Spirit will work in that person's life. He might use someone completely different to lead that person to Christ, such as a relative, a co-worker, a random stranger or another friend. Remember this key verse in 1 Corinthians 3:8. "The one who plants and the one who waters work together with the same purpose. And both will be rewarded for their own hard work" (NLT).

The one who plants and the one who waters work together with the same purpose. And both will be rewarded for their own hard work.

Even if we aren't the person who leads them to Christ, we can be assured that the Holy Spirit will follow up in their lives and work in them if we demonstrate Christ to people.

When I was a child, my mother's neighbor was a Christian, and she started taking my mother to Christian ladies' fellowship meetings once a month. A couple of times a month, this lady looked after me and my three siblings to give my mother some respite and some time to herself.

My mother was amazed that we weren't ever naughty at the neighbor's house. She asked the neighbor, "Why don't my children misbehave at your house?"

The neighbor replied confidently, "Jesus lives here, and children can't act up where Jesus is." My mother was fascinated to hear her say that someone who died 2,000 years ago was living in her house. She went to the fellowship meetings with this woman. Eventually, this woman told my mom, "If you want to know if Jesus is real, just pray and ask him to do something important for you to prove beyond a shadow of a doubt that he exists and that he loves you."

For many years, my older brother had been picking on me and causing me trouble. My older brother had been out of control as a child and was very naughty, and after my mother prayed that prayer to Jesus, my brother stopped picking on me and stopped acting out. His entire behavior changed. He became the same perfect little boy that he was at the neighbor's house. My mother was convinced that Jesus was real and gave her life to Jesus.

She shared part of the reason she gave her life to Jesus with me. She used to have another neighbor some years before that had a few Down's Syndrome children. The mother with the Down's Syndrome children also used to watch us from time to time to give my mother a break. My mother said that this woman was never flustered, and she never seemed stressed. She seemed to handle everything with love and poise, and my mother was impressed with how much she loved all of the children. My mother was impressed with how much she loved her Down's Syndrome children and how she loved my mother's children — my sister and brothers. She knew that this woman was a Christian, and when my mother was making the decision to become a Christian, she considered this friend that she used to have with the Down's Syndrome children. She said to herself, "I want to become like her. I want to live a life of peace and joy and not be flustered, and I want to love my children and other people's children like she does."

This is an example of how this other woman in my mother's life allowed her to become a Christian and to make that decision. I say this because you might not find out that a person that you invested years in at work become a Christian later. They might become a Christian 20 years after you knew them, but no matter when it happens, the Holy Spirit likely used your relationship with them to make an impression on them about what sort of person a Christian is. You likely planted the seeds for their salvation in the time that you spent with them.

Personally, I don't get carried away with how many salvations I help happen; I just make the effort to demonstrate Jesus to everyone that I meet and see. I am full of love and consideration and time for people, and you will understand that as I share the concepts in this book of what I do to demonstrate Jesus. So rest assured, the Holy Spirit knows what he is doing. He knows how to use your example, your love and the time that you're putting into these people to benefit them in the future.

Daily Prayers for People God Brings Across Your Path

Another proactive step that you can take so that people are saved and so that they come into the Kingdom is to write a list of people you know who aren't Christians. Every day, bring their name before the Father and pray for their salvation. I'm very close to my mother who says that she doesn't believe that anyone comes into the Kingdom of God unless someone first prayed for them. Although I am not 100 percent sure of this, I tend to agree with her. In any case, prayer is certainly a big factor in a person's salvation. Take the time each day when you pray to lift up the people that you're doing life with. Not only does that affect the will of God and affect what actually happens in their lives now and in the future, but it also affects the way that you demonstrate your love for these people.

If you have spent time in prayer for people and if you have asked God to bring them to salvation, then this will affect your attitude about how you treat them. Jesus tells us to pray for our enemies. Part of praying for our enemies includes adjusting our feelings about how we consider our enemies. Once you start investing time and praying for your enemies, your attitude changes because you've been spending time in prayer. The same thing is true for the people you care about and the people that you do life with. The more time you spend in prayer for them, the better your relationship will be with them. This will affect how you do life with them and the time and effort you spend into sowing God into them. Pray for people that you're doing life with daily.

Learn to Prophesy or Heal

The gift of prophecy is available for everyone, even for people who are not Pentecostal and who don't believe in the gifts of the Holy Spirit. Even so, prophecy would be hard to do if you don't believe that Jesus can speak today. You might not be able to speak a word from Jesus to someone else if you don't believe that he still speaks today. However, Jesus does still speak today.

For people who have heard from Jesus and who know that he speaks, I have released a book called "Prophetic Evangelism Made Simple" about the gift of prophecy and the ability to share messages from Jesus with people who are not saved. I use this method effectively to sow seeds in people's lives about Jesus and God. He gives me personal messages for people. They are usually short messages since people are busy doing life. When you approach them, you are basically interrupting their day and their activities.

For this reason, you should usually share short messages as a seed. I teach the reasons why prophetic evangelism works in that book. I share how to have the attitude of caring for every person that you minister to. I share a little bit about evangelism in the book and the right attitudes to have when you approach people. I encourage you to buy that book and to learn to prophesy to people. I encourage every reader to share short messages from Jesus with people, which will benefit them.

Once again, do not have any agenda. Every time I prophesy to people, I don't share the Gospel with them, yet I do share the Kingdom with them because that's the Kingdom that comes into people's lives when Jesus speaks to them. I leave their salvation up to the Holy Spirit, and I trust him to lead people to Christ. Learning to prophesy is really effective. Someone can be struggling with something or going through something hard, and whether you know it or not, Jesus has the right words for everyone in every situation.

You can develop the ability to prophesy and bring the words of Jesus to people. This effectively solves people's problems and gives them directions that come straight from God. In addition to the books that I have written, other books also teach you how to prophesy.

I bring up this subject because it's such a big part of my life. Prophetic evangelism is very important to me, and I regularly share with strangers. I prophesy over people in shopping centers, restaurants and wherever I go. I even offer live prophecies on Facebook.

I know a young girl who worked behind the counter at a restaurant. I have encouraged her couple of times with hopeful words. I once told her, "If I ran a café or restaurant, I'd hire you because I know what it means to be a good worker, and you're an extremely good worker."

She was very encouraged by that, and each time I buy a toasted sandwich from her at the shop, she smiles and asks me how I am. She is the type of person that I was starting to get to know. She doesn't have much time to chat because there's always a line of customers. However, I can still affect people like that with who I am. You can look for people like her that you regularly see in the community so that you can impact them as well — a cashier, your barber or hair stylist, a gas station attendant, a waitress and so forth.

I prophesy to a lot to total strangers. This book is essentially about ministering Christ and demonstrating Jesus to people that we know. I gave this example briefly in this book just to let you know that this is one avenue of sharing Christ with others. If you want to buy "Prophetic Evangelism Made Simple," it costs 99 cents on Kindle, or you can order it in paperback.

Another way that you can reach out to people is to learn how to minister healing to others. A great book on this topic is "Divine Healing Made Simple" by Praying Medic, who is a friend of mine. I know him through Facebook and through talking on Skype. He's a really loving person who is very effective in healing. He used to drive an ambulance and minister to people on the job. He prayed for people wherever he went. He not only transported sick people but also healed sick people. He now writes books full time. Reading the book "Divine Healing Made Simple" will really encourage you to embark on a journey of praying for people and seeing them healed.

He has also written two other books, "My Craziest Adventures with God: Part 1" and "My Craziest Adventures with God: Part 2." These two books relate many of his stories of healing in the ambulance and in other places. You can look up Praying Medic on Amazon and check out these books. One of these books really set a spark in me and changed my attitude toward praying for people who are sick. It encouraged me to be bold when I hear someone has a need and to actually step out in faith and pray for the person.

You can demonstrate Christ's kingdom and his power and the fact that he exists today by praying for healing for people and by seeing them healed. What a tremendous example! What an amazing way for you to demonstrate Jesus as you pray for healing for a person that you're doing life with. They can be suffering with an illness or injury, and you can come alongside them and pray for them. Their healing will really influence them and give them a great opinion of Jesus Christ and Christianity.

I recommend that you buy the book "Divine Healing Made Simple" by Praying Medic and encourage you to learn how to pray for healing for others. In the Gospels, in the Great Commission, we are to cast out demons and heal the sick. Instead, many people are trying to preach and demonstrate the Gospel without healing. Some of the best evangelists in the world have the gifts of healing and can pray for people in the audience. You can impact many people if you learn to personally walk in the gift of healing and grow in the knowledge, wisdom and ability to heal people. Thus, you can effectively demonstrate Jesus and his Kingdom to people.

Invite Your Friends to Evangelistic Outreaches

Sometimes, evangelists visit your city. They might not come to your church, but you might hear about them visiting through social media. Pay attention to when special speakers come and ask God for his leading about who can you invite. You can effectively lead people to Christ and influence them at these events. If you've invested time into a person and listened to them for hours and helped them move or watched their children or done some of the other things that I have talked about in this book, then they might be open to attending an evangelistic event with you.

You can tell them that a special speaker is coming to your church or to another venue and ask them if they want to come. Most often, people politely accept your invitation. Evangelists have the anointing, the power of God, to release and demonstrate the Christian faith, and they are very convincing. They have the Holy Spirit's power on their words, and they effectively win souls and people to Jesus Christ. They speak with authority from the pulpit, and your friend might really respect them and be influenced by an evangelist.

My brother's wife wasn't a Christian, but her friend knew the Lord. The second woman often shared with my sister-in-law and demonstrated Jesus to her as a loving friend. One time, this friend took her to an evangelistic meeting, and my brother's wife became a Christian. People are still saved at these types of meetings today. God regularly uses evangelists to win souls to his Kingdom. Take advantage of an evangelist's gifts when they come to town.

Even so, most of the work will be done by you as you sow seeds in the person's life, like the story I shared about my sister. She spent 10 years being friends with these two families before she shared the Gospel with them over six weeks. When did they become Christians? Over the six weeks or over the 10 years as my sister invested her time? You've done most of the hard work by being a friend to a person and investing your time in them. When you take them to an evangelist, and they become a Christian, just know that 90 percent of the work was done by you, and only 10 percent was done by the evangelist.

Take advantage of opportunities when an evangelist comes to town. If you have many friends that you do life with regularly, and if you're developing deeper friendships with them, you should be aware of evangelistic meetings and their schedules.

Give Powerful Books to Your Friends

You can read solid books that demonstrate Jesus and his life, books that will help you understand the Christian faith. I strongly recommend that you buy the following two books:

"Beyond Justice" by Joshua Graham is a crime fiction drama.

You can read the back cover on Amazon, which says:

"THE DESCENT INTO HELL IS NOT ALWAYS VERTICAL... Sam Hudson, a reputable San Diego attorney, learns this when the authorities wrongfully convict him of the brutal rape and murder of his wife and daughter, and sends him to death row. There he awaits execution by lethal injection. If he survives that long. In prison, Sam fights for his life while his attorney works frantically on his appeal. It is then that he embraces the faith of his departed wife and begins to manifest supernatural abilities. Abilities which help him save lives — his own, those of his unlikely allies — and uncover the true killer's identity, unlocking the door to his exoneration. Now a free man, Sam's newfound faith confronts him with the most insurmountable challenge yet. A challenge beyond vengeance, beyond rage, beyond anything Sam believes himself capable of: to forgive the very man who murdered his family, according to his faith. But this endeavor reveals darker secrets than either Sam or the killer could ever have imagined. Secrets that hurtle them into a fateful collision course. BEYOND JUSTICE, a tale of loss, redemption, and forgiveness."[2]

It's a beautiful Christian story and one that would be interesting for someone to read who is not a Christian as it really demonstrates the Christian message to them. That's on my list of books to give to people who aren't Christians since it's a book that would witness to them.

Another book that I recommend is called "Redeeming Love" by Francine Rivers.

The back cover as seen on Amazon says:

"A Story of Love That Won't Let Go - No Matter What!

---

[2]https://www.amazon.com/Beyond-Justice-Joshua-Graham/dp/0984452605/ref=sr_1_1?s=books&ie=UTF8&qid=1480800594&sr=1-1&keywords=beyond+justice+by+joshua+graham

California's gold country, 1850. A time when men sold their souls for a bag of gold and women sold their bodies for a place to sleep.

Angel expects nothing from men but betrayal. Sold into prostitution as a child, she survives by keeping her hatred alive. And what she hates most are the men who use her, leaving her empty and dead inside.

Then she meets Michael Hosea, a man who seeks his Father's heart in everything. Michael obeys God's call to marry Angel and to love her unconditionally. Slowly, day by day, he defies Angel's every bitter expectation, until despite her resistance, her frozen heart begins to thaw.

But with her unexpected softening comes overwhelming feelings of unworthiness and fear. And so Angel runs. Back to the darkness, away from her husband's pursuing love, terrified of the truth she no longer can deny: Her final healing must come from the One who loves her even more than Michael does…the One who will never let her go.

A powerful retelling of the story of Gomer and Hosea, Redeeming Love is a life-changing story of God's unconditional, redemptive, all-consuming love."[3]

So as you read books, you can find ones to encourage people who aren't Christians to give them. You can pick the

---

[3]https://www.amazon.com/Redeeming-Love-Francine-Rivers/dp/1590525132/ref=sr_1_1?s=books&ie=UTF8&qid=1480800657&sr=1-1&keywords=redeeming+love+by+francine+rivers

right time during a conversation with people to give them a book that would influence them and lead them closer to Jesus.

I have written a very evangelistic book called "Michael Jackson Speaks from Heaven," an interview with Michael Jackson. In it, he shares what life in heaven is like and the fact that the only way into heaven is through Jesus.

Simply Share the Gospel

You can read books on how to share the Gospel simply. I shared about "Christianity Explained," an evangelistic course. Here is the link to the website: http://www.christianityexplained.com.

Look for books on sharing the Gospel. You can learn how to reach others for Jesus, and then, at the right time, with consultation from God, you can share with them. Ask God about whether it is the right time to share with one of your friends and ask him to give you his peace about the situation. Let peace, not anxiety, guide you about the situation. Let God demonstrate the peace through you that he wants you to share.

Of course, if you speak to God and if you prophesy, you want to hear him say, "Yes! I want you to share the gospel with _____ (insert friend's name) today. "

You need to have that confirmation directly from God. I encourage you to learn how to share the Gospel. Remember that you might only share the Gospel with your friend after years of friendship. You might only have one shot for 15 minutes over the course of years.

A number of times, my mother tried to share the Gospel with her mother who was a white witch. My mother would finish the presentation, and her mother would say, "I'm not interested." One time, her mother said to her after she shared the Gospel again, "I know that you want me to believe in this. I understand what you're saying about Jesus, but I've got no interest in having him be the Savior of my life. I know I could pretend and say to you that I accept Jesus, and it would make you happy. But that would be lying, and lying is against who I am."

This really upset my mother. The first time she shared the Gospel with her, she wasn't deterred from sharing it the second time. However, my grandma told her this the second time that my mother shared with her. Well, a few years passed, and my grandma grew close to death. Once again, my mother shared the Gospel with her mother. She remembered what her mother had said about not wanting to know Jesus. However, this time, the last time when she shared the Gospel with her mother, her mother was very happy to accept Jesus.

She reached this last stage in her life, and she was ready to accept Jesus. Not long after that, my grandma passed away and went to heaven. I've been able to be updated by Jesus on how my grandmother is doing in heaven. I am excited to know that she is in heaven. My mother learned how to share the Gospel with someone. You should also learn how to share the Gospel and pick the right verses to share so that you can do it in 15 minutes. It doesn't take a lot of time. You can share the essentials that will bring conviction to them.

Even so, you might not be the one that shares the Gospel with your friend, like I have said before. If you're praying for them every night and if you've got a love relationship with them, God will make a way for them somehow.

If you're open to Jesus and to Holy Spirit, the Holy Spirit might tell you that he wants you to share the gospel with a person. This would be your opportunity to spend that 15 minutes sharing with the person.

Read Resources on how to Share the Gospel

I've already covered buying a book and resources that will teach you how to share the Gospel. Just think for a moment about spending eternity in hell and how gruesome and terrible that would be. Think about the people that you do life with and friends from work and people that you love who aren't Christians. Imagine them being there and then consider what that is worth. Is it worth you embarrassing yourself? Is it worth you taking a risk and sharing the Gospel with your friend? Is it worth the little bit of fear or anxiety you might feel about bringing up the subject of Christianity and sharing the Gospel with someone?

If your fear is stopping them from going to eternal damnation, is it worth it to you? Consider them spending eternity in burning flames. Invest in resources on learning how to share the Gospel and demonstrate Jesus to people that you love.

Pray from Your Friend's Perspective

When you talk to your friend and spend time with them, be sure to ask them questions about their life and what they're going through. Based on information from your friend about how they feel about a certain situation, take those issues to prayer.

God cares about everyone. He doesn't just care about people who are Christians. He will work and intervene in people's lives that aren't Christians. He answers prayers for people who do not profess Christianity. People who aren't of the Christian faith can reach out to God and pray, and he answers prayers and leads people to himself.

Find out how your friends are feeling. Then, put yourself in that situation so that you're feeling the same emotions and pray on their behalf, interceding for them according to what you are sensing. This will have an effect on them, and you will be able to see God working in situations and in their lives. Similar to my mother's neighbor, tell people who are considering Christ to ask God for something that's important to them to happen. Tell people to ask God to intervene and see what happens when they've got a situation that they can't deal with or can't handle.

Tell them, "When you prove God exists and that he does care for you, then you can give your life to him." I often tell the strangers that I meet to put God to the test. I tell them to reach out to him and ask him to intervene in the situations of life.

It says in the Bible in Romans 10:13, "Everyone who calls on the name of the Lord will be saved." That passage is quoted from the Old Testament. The Old Testament says "all that call upon the Lord God shall be saved," but the New Testament refers to Jesus instead of the Lord God. If you can stir up people in conversation to ask God for help, then you put them in a position where God can intervene and demonstrate that he loves them.

If you talk to people and begin to understand how they are feeling, come alongside them and pray for God to intervene in their situation, according to their needs.

Introduce your Friends to Other Christians

Some people have non-Christian friends in one part of their lives and have their Christian friends in another part of their lives, and the two groups of friends don't mix. You might think about having one of your Christian friends from church come to your workplace for lunch and invite one of your friends from work to lunch to meet your Christian friend. When people who aren't saved yet meet your friends that are saved, they can see another example of a beautiful and loving person that knows Jesus. You want to present evidence that Jesus Christ is alive and that he cares for your friend. One of the ways you can do that is to introduce your Christian friend to your non-Christian friend.

The more they interconnect, the more they can cross-pollinate each other and the more impact the relationship will have on others. Thus, the Holy Spirit can use the circumstance to speak to your non-Christian friend. On the one hand, don't be afraid of your friends at church and don't be afraid of hiding your non-Christian friends from church. Don't worry that your Christian friends are going to say something that will offend your non-Christian friend.

If you are really open and allow your friends to connect with each other, you might find that your Christian friend has more influence on your friend than you do when it comes to giving their life to Jesus. This is what happened with my brother's wife who became friends with one of his friends, and that woman then ministered to my sister-in-law. She shared life with my sister-in-law and loved her and took her to an evangelistic meeting where she was eventually saved. She was saved through my brother's friend, not through anything that my brother did. One of the keys to the salvation of your non-Christian friends might be one of your Christian friends who impacts the non-Christian.

Don't worry if your Christian friend from church becomes good friends with people that you know that aren't from church. Don't be afraid if these people develop a friendship and start to go out without you. Trust that Jesus knows what he is doing and actively encourage your friends to mix and cross-pollinate like a bee goes from flower to flower, fertilizing each flower with the pollen from the previous flower. Encourage your friends to connect with each other because it really helps your non-Christian friends.

Include Them in Your Christian Groups

Treat your non-Christian friends as though they're Christians. When your Christian friends are getting together for a New Year's Eve party or birthday or any celebration, ask your friends from work to come. Invite the people that you know that aren't Christians to the Christian gatherings. Just act like it's not offensive to your non-Christian friend to go to Christian gatherings. Invite them along as though they fit in and act as if it's natural for them to be included. Don't assume that there is a big gap between your non-Christian friends and your Christian friends and don't have an agenda.

Don't invite them just so that they get saved but include your non-Christian friends in the celebrations and get-togethers of your Christian friends. As I shared, my mother's next-door neighbor took her to Christian women's gatherings and other meetings before my mother eventually got saved. My mother told me that she used to like to go into the kitchen at these gatherings and wash up, and she used to like to hear the Christian women talking. She told me that the Christian women talked as though Jesus was alive, that he didn't die 2,000 years ago but that he was actually living and involved in their lives. Their conversations fascinated my mother.

My mother believed that Jesus was dead, yet these women were talking as though he was alive and part of their lives. Their words strongly influenced my mother, and she started to wonder whether she, too, could have a relationship with this living Jesus. Don't have an agenda as your non-Christian friends meet your Christian friends. Don't try to force the issue or make all your Christian friends be on their best behavior. Just include your friends, and let the Holy Spirit take control. The relationship will flow naturally.

One of your Christian friends might offend your friend, which can be tough. You can talk to your non-Christian friend and say that people are human and just because you are Christian, doesn't mean you're perfect. Satan does have a role to play in a person's life; he does affect Christians and non-Christians but just be assured that the Holy Spirit knows what he's doing. The Holy Spirit understands your non-Christian friend. The Holy Spirit has watched your non-Christian friend through all their life. He knows what interests your non-Christian friend. He knows what will affect your friend; he knows how to witness and how to demonstrate Jesus to your friend. So relax and just invite non-Christians and connect your friends as you watch the Holy Spirit go to work on them.

Even if your non-Christian friend and your Christian friend connect for years without your non-Christian friend becoming saved, they have still been immersed in the Christian culture. They are not offended by Christians, which is part of the process of becoming a Christian. If your non-Christian friends like to hang out with Christians, let it be!

I have repeated a number of times in this book that you should not have an agenda, but you should just let the Holy Spirit take control in the relationships.

Ask God to Open Your Friend's Heart to Your Faith

You can be sure that the Holy Spirit is working in a person's life when they start to ask questions about your faith. The Holy Spirit is very good at speaking to a person's mind, Christian or not. The Holy Spirit is very good at talking to your friend and putting questions in his or her mind about your Christian faith and your life and your walk with God. If you pray for your friend and ask God to pique your friend's interest so that he or she asks questions about your faith, you will have an opportunity to share your testimony and your faith with your friend.

You can ask God specifically to work in the life of your non-Christian friend so that they ask questions about your faith. When they do start asking questions, you have an opportunity to share your testimony and even to share the Gospel with your friend.

When They Make a Decision for Jesus, Disciple Them

You can buy books on discipleship. My mother has a whole course of 10 lessons that she has developed herself, and she used these in her church to disciple people. Make sure that you buy a book or a resource that describes the fundamentals of the Christian faith. They are the key points that you believe, but you can't necessarily share these with a person off the top of your head. Make sure you buy a resource on Christian discipleship. You can easily find one on Amazon and buy the book or manual. Go through each of the lessons to make sure that the person is properly discipled.

Please do this so that the person grows in their faith. Many people become Christians, and when life becomes too hard for them, they fall away. In the parable of the Sower and the Seed, Jesus talked about four types of seeds:

Seed falling on hard ground with birds taking away the seed

Seed falling into a little soil that dries up

Seed falling into ground with weeds that choke out the seed and

Seed that sees a hundred-fold increase.

Jesus shared that parable to make the point that even when someone hears the Word, it might not take root. They fall away, and their faith might die. When you sow the Word into your friend, give them a solid foundation for their Christian faith.

Two days ago, my brother's roommate asked him his opinion about what sort of person the roommate was. My brother asked him if he was sure that he wanted to hear the opinion because it would hurt. The roommate told him that he wanted to know the answer. My brother spoke freely and told him that he is arrogant, hypocritical and addressed a few subjects. My brother complained, "For instance, you say you believe in evolution so that I can't talk to my friends. I can't play my YouTube videos about Christian topics or host Christian activities. But have you ever considered this?"

He then showed his roommate a 15-minute message on YouTube about creation, which totally destroyed this guy's faith in evolution. Now, the roommate wants to know about the Christian faith and become a Christian. You will need to be there at the right time. My brother was very encouraged to see this guy totally turnaround from being a really staunch atheist and a staunch believer in evolution to becoming open to the Christian faith. Similarly, it will be exciting for you to lead one of your friends to Jesus. I am sure that you will be thrilled to see one of your friends in the Kingdom of God and to know that they're going to heaven.

That's just the very beginning of the journey that you will have with your friend, and once your friend becomes a Christian, they will be able to be friends with your Christian friends. Hopefully, you already introduced them to other Christians, and they are friends already.

Please understand that the purpose of becoming friends with people and investing time in them is to lead them to Jesus so that they know him. Don't be upset if your friendship moves away from being as close as it was at one point if your friend actually spends more time with one of your Christian friends.

Don't be afraid if your friend finds a boyfriend or girlfriend and begins a relationship with another Christian or if he or she leaves your workplace or moves out of state. Don't worry if you grow apart. Hold on to the happy memories that are part of your friend becoming a Christian. Trust that God will sustain your friend and help him or her grow.

In this book, I address how I interact with others and how I share my faith with them. When I was talking about this book to my mother today, she observed, "People need to know that not everyone is like you, Matthew, and they cannot always do things the way that you do them."

You should realize that some of the things that I shared might be really hard for you to do while other things I shared might come really easily. In any case, we've got to be light and be part of the solution and not worry so much about what's going on in the world. We've got to provide the answers, to be light and salt of this earth. It's exciting to be a Christian and to connect with many people like I am. I encourage you to do that also. Before I close, I'll pray a prayer for you and finish the book.

"Dear Father, I pray for everyone who buys this book and reads it. I pray that they would all become effective witnesses for you. I pray that you would be with this reader. I pray that they would be able to understand the material in this book. I pray for a special release and anointing to come on them. I pray for your presence to be manifest and go with them. I pray that they can read this book and glean for themselves the treasures that are in it and follow the advice that I recommend in it. I pray that they can go and demonstrate you, demonstrate Jesus to this world effectively. I pray personally for the friends that these people have that are non-Christians. May you shine your light in their lives and manifest yourself to them. I pray that your Holy Spirit would work in the lives of the non-Christian people that these readers know. I pray that you would have your will and way in the readers and change the readers and give them boldness and courage to share your message with people that they know. May they share you with others and pour out your love on people that they know in better and more effective ways as outlined in this book. In Jesus' Name I ask. Amen!"

God bless you and keep you!

Closing Thoughts

I have read this book three times to partially edit it before I send it to my editor to polish. I realize that I have covered a lot of material in these pages. This book is different from my other books because it does not have chapters but instead has subject headings. I am happy with this format in hindsight as I can see that many of you will have to refer back to this book from time to time. Each of the subjects is highlighted and linked up on the Kindle version. Each page number is listed in the table of contents of the paperback so that you have a quick reference to refer to when you need a refresher.

This might not be the most exhaustive book that you might read on evangelism, yet I can personally say that I don't think I could have written a better book about this subject. For years, I have wanted to share with people how I approach evangelism and really, how I approach life.

Over the past 16 years, I have given about 10,000 prophetic messages to strangers I have encountered on the streets of Sydney. In addition, I have had just as many conversations with people on public transport where I have sown the seeds of the Gospel. My whole life purpose is to lead people to Christ that don't know him and to lead Christians into a closer and more intimate relationship with Jesus.

I live to impact people for the Kingdom.

I am confident that if you study this book and put it into practice, you will see effective fruit in the lives of the people that you do life with. It is an honor for me to spend $1,500 to have this book edited and published. That money is worth it to me even if only one of you becomes as effective as I am at sharing Jesus.

Here are some highlights of my life.

On one day, I gave 20 prophetic words to strangers, led five people to the Lord and led one backslidden person back to the Lord.

One day, while I was on public transport, I led three separate people to the Lord at different times of the day.

On one admission to a mental hospital, I led a backslidden man back to Jesus and opened his spiritual eyes so that he met Jesus and angels in visons while I was there. During that same hospital stay, I had a schizophrenic "hear" God for me and give me a message from him like my gay friend did. When God finished speaking though her, she asked me how she could hear God all the time. She told me it was the most beautiful and peaceful voice she had ever heard. I led her to Jesus right then and there.

I have impacted many people throughout my life, and I pray that you, too, will become like me.

God bless you.

Matthew Robert Payne

November 2016.

I'd love to hear from you

One of the ways that you can bless me as a writer is by writing an honest and candid review of my book on Amazon. I always read the reviews of my books, and I would love to hear what you have to say about this one.

Before I buy a book, I read the reviews first. You can make an informed decision about a book when you have read enough honest reviews from readers. One way to help me sell this book and to give me positive feedback is by writing a review for me. It doesn't cost you a thing but helps me and the future readers of this book enormously.

To sow into my book writing ministry, to read my blog or to request a life coaching session or your own personal prophecy from God, you can visit http://personal-prophecy-today.com. All of your gifts will go toward the books that I write and self-publish.

To write to me about this book or any other thoughts, please feel free to contact me at my personal email address at survivors.sanctuary@gmail.com.

You can also friend request me on Facebook at Matthew Robert Payne. Please send me a message if we have no friends in common as a lot of scammers now send me friend requests.

You can also do me a huge favor and share this book on Facebook as a recommended book to read. This will help me and other readers.

Other Books by Matthew Robert Payne

The Parables of Jesus Made Simple

The Prophetic Supernatural Experience

Prophetic Evangelism Made Simple

Your Identity in Christ

His Redeeming Love- A Memoir

Writing and Self-Publishing Christian Nonfiction

Coping with your Pain and Suffering

Living for Eternity

Jesus Speaking Today

Great Cloud of Witnesses Speak

My Radical Encounters with Angels

Finding Intimacy with Jesus Made Simple

My Radical Encounters with Angels- Book Two

A Beginner's Guide to the Prophetic

Michael Jackson Speaks from Heaven

7 Keys to Intimacy with Jesus

Conversations with God Book 1

Optimistic Visions of Revelation

Conversations with God Book 2

Finding Your Purpose in Christ

Coming Soon:

My Visits to the Galactic Council of Heaven

Deep Calls unto Deep: Common Questions about the Prophetic

You can find my published books on my Amazon author page here: http://tinyurl.com/jq3h893

About the Author

Matthew was raised in a Baptist church and was led to the Lord at the tender age of 8. He has experienced some pain and darkness in his life, which has given him a deep compassion and love for all people.

Today, he runs two Facebook groups, one called "Open Heavens and Intimacy with Jesus" and one called "Prophetic Training Group." Matthew has a commission from the Lord to train up prophets and to mentor others in the Christian faith. He does this through his groups and by writing relevant books for the Christian faith.

God has commissioned him to write at least 50 books in his life, and he spends his days writing and earning the money to self-publish. You can support him by donating money at http://personal-prophecy-today.com or by requesting your own personal prophecy or life coaching session.

It is Matthew's prayer that this book has blessed you, and he hopes it will lead you to increased boldness and to win some of your friends for Christ.

www.ingramcontent.com/pod-product-compliance
Lightning Source LLC
Chambersburg PA
CBHW052054070526
44584CB00017B/2180